Leatherwork

Anne and Jane Cope

Leatherwork

photography by John Warren   line drawings by Jane Cope

Pan Original Pan Books London and Sydney

Our thanks to Andy Dill and Martha Stanley for
modelling some of the articles in the colour photographs.

First published 1979 by Pan Books Ltd,
Cavaye Place, London SW10 9PG
© Anne and Jane Cope 1979
ISBN 0 330 25839 7
Printed and bound in Great Britain by
Butler & Tanner Ltd, Frome, Somerset

Contents

About this book

We've divided this book into two parts. The first half, really the guts of the subject, describes all the hand tools and techniques associated with leatherwork. In the second half we describe how various items are made; you'll find most of the techniques discussed in the first half illustrated here. We really don't expect you to read the book straight through. Flick through the early chapters just to see what leatherwork is all about, then go straight to the section on belts, clothes or whatever you want to make and find out which tools and techniques are involved. Then turn back to the relevant chapters and have a really careful read.

The range of items we designed and made for this book reflect our feeling that while leather is undoubtedly tops for things like belts, bags and footgear it definitely deserves wider use. We've not included small items like purses, comb cases, bookmarks or key-ring tabs simply because with the basic know-how gleaned from the first part of the book you'll find they're really no problem.

In all honesty we can't say it's always cheaper to make your own leather gear. By the time you've bought the tools and the leather to make a belt, say, you're well on the way to paying more than the price of a bought one. On the other hand if you make two belts, or three or four, the economics begin to look a lot healthier. The moral is to make several items from the same leather using the same tools. There again, money-saving probably won't be your prime motivation. Leather is a superb natural material – it looks good, feels good and smells good – in short it has intrinsic quality and that's what really counts.

Not so long ago leatherwork was a rather esoteric occupation. Well, now there are more places to get tools from and more erstwhile trade-only suppliers willing to sell to individuals like you and us. A dozen or so suppliers of leather and tools are listed in the Appendix.

We can remember very well the kinds of things which puzzled us to begin with. So we hope this book will answer for you what only became clear to us after a fair amount of trial and error and piecing together of advice from various sources.

part one
Working with leather

1 Leather

How leather is prepared

Slaughtering an animal and putting it in cold storage as a skinned, cleaned carcass takes less than fifteen minutes in a modern abattoir. The raw hide or skin, salted to delay putrefaction, is sent to a tannery. Before tanning it is unhaired, fleshed, washed to remove the chemicals used in unhairing, and pickled. Pickling makes it receptive to tanning agents. If left untanned a skin will rot, just like meat. Tanning is the process which turns a skin or hide into the durable substance we know as leather. So, by definition, leather isn't leather until it has been tanned.

Today nine out of ten skins are mineral tanned, usually with chromium salts. 'Chrome tanning', as it is called in the trade, is a fast, modern method which produces soft, resilient leathers ideal for shoe uppers, gloves and clothing. Aniline dyes give vibrant colours on this sort of leather. Vegetable tanning, with the natural tannins found in wood, bark, leaves or seed pods, is a much older and slower method, and gives a denser tannage. Vegetable tanned leather feels slippery when it is wet. It also holds creases, stamping or moulding better than the chrome-tanned variety. There are also combination tanning processes, involving both vegetable and mineral tanning agents. Some leathers, chamois for example, are produced by tanning with oils and fats.

After tanning comes splitting or shaving to the desired thickness, then dyeing, then 'fat liquoring' to put back the natural oils lost in tanning, then various smoothing, stretching, flexing and rolling processes, then perhaps buffing and the application of films to impart stain and scuff resistance, then 'plating' or ironing, then perhaps embossing, and finally grading, measuring, rolling into bundles or draping over 'horses'. After that it takes a canny customer to know just what he is looking at. Not all leathers undergo all these processes of course.

Structure of leather

Leather is a unique material. Makers of synthetics have tried to imitate it, even to the point of impregnating their products with leather smell, and failed. Leather owes its porosity, flexibility, plasticity and low thermal conductivity to its two-layered structure.

The side on which the wool or hair grew is known as the grain layer. This is usually fairly thin, less than a quarter of the thickness of the skin. It merges into a much thicker layer, the layer next to the flesh or meat of the animal, which has a honeycomb structure. If you looked at this layer under a powerful microscope you would see that it is composed of bundles of fibres intricately woven together in all directions. At even greater magnification you would see that each fibre is itself a collection of finer fibres or fibrils. In between the fibre bundles there are tiny channels which allow the passage of air and water vapour. It is the state of this fibrous layer, compressed or filled with oils and other substances during tanning, which determines the quality of the leather.

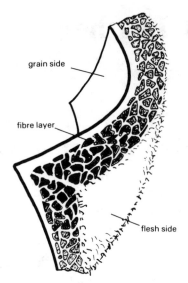

Leather terms

Leather has its fair share of technical terms. If you have to interpret mail order catalogues or want to nod intelligently at warehousemen you'll find the next few paragraphs helpful. All the larger mammals – cattle, horses, camels – have *hides* rather than skins. Cattle hides are sold whole or divided in the following ways:

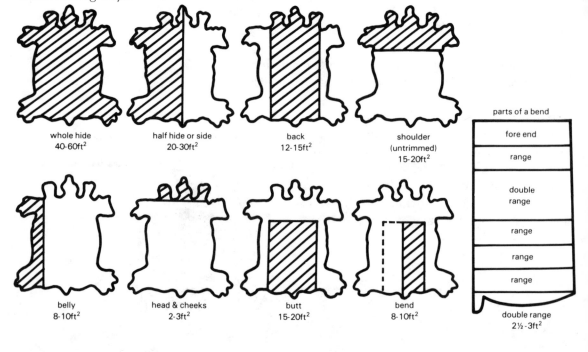

whole hide
40-60ft^2

half hide or side
20-30ft^2

back
12-15ft^2

shoulder
(untrimmed)
15-20ft^2

belly
8-10ft^2

head & cheeks
2-3ft^2

butt
15-20ft^2

bend
8-10ft^2

parts of a bend

fore end

range

double range

range

range

range

double range
2½-3ft^2

Sheep, goats, pigs and all smaller animals have *skins*. Before they are split or shaved all skins and hides have a *grain side*, the side from which the hair or wool was removed, and a *flesh side*, the side from which flesh was removed. A *grain leather* is one with the grain side substantially intact. A *full grain leather* is much the same only more so! Natural grain patterns tend to be most marked in the shoulder area. Pigskin, of course, has an attractive grain all over. In some leathers the grain is partially removed by abrasion, a process called 'frizing' or buffing.

Thick leather may be split into two or more layers before tanning. The grain layer or top layer is known as the *grain split* or *top split*, and the underlying layers as *middle splits* and *bottom* or *flesh splits*.

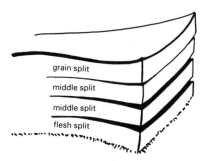

Grain splits may be finished for wear on the grain side or flesh side. Very often the back of grain leather is just as usable as the grain side. This is why grain leathers such as garment cowhide and nappa (see pages 15–16) are such good value.

Middle or flesh splits are sueded, or velvety, on both sides. *Suede* in fact describes any leather which has been buffed to a fine 'nap' or pile on one or both sides. A suede split is sueded on both sides, though one side may be fuzzier than the other.

Any skin or hide which has not been split or shaved is described as *full sheep*, *full hide*, etc.

Though it may seem academic, there is an important difference between 'split' used as an adjective and 'split' used as a noun. In other words split cowhide is not the same as cowhide split. Split used as an adjective, as in split cowhide, denotes a grain split; but split used as a noun, as in cowhide split, denotes a flesh or middle split. Don't send off for split cowhide expecting to receive something sueded on both sides.

You should now be able to work out what leather sides and sueded sides are. Both terms can occur in catalogues, meaning grain splits finished for wear on the grain side and flesh side respectively. A sueded side makes better quality suede clothing than a flesh split. 'Side' automatically means one is talking about cow or cattle hide (see page 14).

Other terms in common use have fairly obvious meanings. *Tooling hide*, for instance, is simply thick natural vegetable tanned cattle hide which responds well to carving, stamping and dyeing. *Bridle leather* and *harness leather* are thick 'curried' leathers that are waterproofed and given great tensile strength by oil or grease treatments after tanning.

Case hide is generally firm dressed split cowhide with a glossy finish, excellent for stiff items such as briefcases and suitcases. *Bag hide* is much more flexible, sometimes embossed with a grain pattern, and used for luggage and handbags. If something is described as 'embossed' you can be sure the grain is an imitation one.

Gloving leather, lining leather, hatband leather, metallized leather, pearlized leather are exactly what they imply. *Coach hide* is a bit of a catch, though; it's actually full grain, 'boarded' vegetable tanned cattle hide used in the handbag and travel goods trade, and nothing to do with coaches. Boarding, by the way, is the process of folding a leather grain to grain and working the fold across the leather to crease and enhance the natural grain.

Kinds of leather and their uses

Don't be put off by the next page or so. In theory your choice of leather is endless. In practice it is limited by the shop or warehouse you buy from.

We've skipped exotic leathers such as lizard, snake, crocodile, turtle, ostrich, frog, toad, shark, whale, elephant, camel, because they're not easy to obtain, expensive and because frankly they look better on their original owners. Believe it or not, even plaice skins – the dark side with the orange spots – are tanned!

The leathers you'll encounter most often come from domestic cattle, sheep, goats and pigs.

Cattle hide In the strict sense any leather made from the hide of a mature bovine animal (cow, ox, steer, bull, buffalo) is 'cattle hide'. As distinctions between cowhide, bull hide, steer hide, etc. are not very useful here, we've homed in on cowhide because it is the most readily obtainable.

Cowhide Strictly this is leather made from the hide of a mature female bovine, but loosely it is synonymous with the hide of any mature bovine. If one talks simply about 'hide' or 'cowhide' one is understood to mean stiffish natural vegetable tanned cowhide, the sort suitable for tooling and making belts rather than the thin flexible sort used for garments. The commonest leathers made from cowhide are these:

Vegetable tanned cowhide This is either the unsplit hide or a grain split; usually 1–4mm thick; stiff or bendy, matt or glossy grain side, natural flesh colour or stained, smooth or fuzzy on flesh side; sold as whole hides, also as sides, backs, bellies, etc. (see page 12); depending on thickness used for soft and hard luggage, belts, seating, tooling and carving, also many industrial purposes

Tooling cowhide This is natural (i.e. creamy or pinkish) vegetable tanned cowhide with a matt grain side, and a fair degree of flexibility, produced specially for carving, tooling and dyeing; sold as whole hides, sides, shoulders, backs and bellies (see page 12); used for belts, bags, or decorative panels

Latigo cowhide The unsplit hide or grain split tanned with aluminium salts and gambier; normally yellow in colour; 1–4mm thick; softer and waxier than the vegetable tanned variety; sold as whole hides, sides, shoulders, etc. (see page 12); used for saddlery, sandals, belts and bags

Garment cowhide The chrome tanned grain split; 0·8–1·5mm thick; natural or dyed (dye may or may not penetrate entire thickness); soft and supple; sold as whole hides or sides (see page 12); for clothing, some bags and other accessories, some upholstery (thicker chrome tanned grain splits are used for shoe uppers, handbags and luggage)

Upholstery cowhide Chrome or vegetable tanned grain split: 1–2mm thick; natural and dyed; various finishes and imitation grains; firmer than garment cowhide; sold as whole hides or sides (see page 12); for furniture and car upholstery

Cowhide split Commonly understood to be the flesh or middle split (not the grain split), sueded both sides, 0·6–1·5mm thick; natural or dyed (dye penetrates entire thickness); soft and velvety; sold as whole hides, sides or bends (see page 12); for clothing, accessories, cushions

Buck or buckskin Strictly speaking this is oil tanned frized grain leather made from deerskin, but sometimes from cowhide; 1–1·5mm thick; fine nap; very soft; used for clothing

Sole leather The vegetable tanned full hide or grain split; 3–8mm thick; sold as bends or ranges (see page 12); for soles and moulded articles

Kip Any leather made from immature European or American cattle, or from smaller Asian or African cattle; 1–2·5mm thick; whole hide 15–25ft²; obtainable unsplit (handbags, travel goods, shoe uppers) and in grain and flesh splits of various thicknesses (garments, bags, linings)

Calf Leather made from an immature bovine; 1–1·5mm thick; whole skin 5–12ft²; unsplit and finished on the grain side (box calf and willow calf) for handbags and shoe uppers; when finished on flesh side known as suede calf or hunting calf

Sheep leather This is leather made from the skin of a sheep or lamb. Skins are sold as whole skins only and may be 3–10ft² depending on the age of the animal. These are some of the commoner sheep leathers:

Nappa Full grain unsplit mineral tanned sheep or lamb skin (also goat or kid); 1–1·25mm thick; many colours, dyed throughout thickness; soft and supple; for clothing, gloves, accessories; a good all-purpose leather

Cabretta Leather from South American hair sheep (i.e. not the woolly kind) finished on the grain or flesh side; 1–1·25mm thick; soft but has less 'body' than nappa; used for gloves, shoe uppers, accessories

Cape Grain leather from South African or other hair sheep; 0·8–1mm thick; very soft and stretchy; for gloves and some clothing

Skiver Grain split of lamb or sheep skin (sometimes goat); 0·6–1mm thick; for linings and bookbinding

Chamois The oil tanned flesh split or frized grain split of sheep or lamb skin (sometimes goat); 0·4–1mm thick; 3–5ft²; very soft and absorbent; used as wash leather, linings and some clothing

Doeskin The aldehyde tanned flesh split of lamb or sheep skin (nothing to do with does nowadays); usually white or cream; very fine nap; 3–5ft²; for gloves and linings

Goat leather This is leather made from the skin of a goat or kid. A whole goat skin measures 3–10ft² depending on the age of the animal. Thickness is usually 0·5–1·25mm. Apart from nappa goat and chamois goat your choice is likely to be limited to:

Morocco Vegetable tanned grain leather boarded to emphasize grain, usually with glossy finish; many colours; for bookbinding, fancy goods

Niger Grain goat leather (sometimes sheep) tanned in Nigeria; for bookbinding, small leather goods

Kid Chrome tanned grain leather from a goat or kid; for shoe uppers, gloves and linings depending on thickness

Pig leather The term 'pigskin' is usually understood to mean vegetable tanned grain leather from a pig of any age. Skin sizes are from 6–12ft^2 and thickness from 0·6–2mm. Pigskin has a characteristically looser fibre structure than sheep or goat leather, and a very distinctive grain (bristle holes arranged in groups of three). It is widely used in the clothing, shoe, handbag and glove trade. You may also encounter:

Hogskin Grain leather made from the peccary (see below) or carpincho (a South American rodent); used for wallets, bags, shoe uppers, trimmings

Peccary Grain leather from South American wild boar (also designated as hogskin); for gloves, bags, trimmings

Pig splits or pig suede The sueded flesh split; for lined belts and small leathergoods

Again, don't be deterred by the technicalities or by the apparent breadth of choice. Just to reassure you, almost all of the articles photographed in this book can be made from natural vegetable tanned cowhide, nappa, garment cowhide or cowhide splits. For every item we have suggested the kind of leather most suitable.
So why bother with the mysteries of Morocco or cabretta? Well, you'll probably come across them at some time, as we did, either in a warehouse or in a catalogue. They may be the only choice you have. A quick way to get to know the feel and uses of various leathers is to have a good snoop round a leathergoods shop.

Quantities and thickness

The leather trade in the UK, and in almost every other country in the world, operates in square feet. A figure 15 stamped or chalked in the corner of a skin or hide means that it measures 15ft². Fractions of a square foot, ¼, ½ and ¾, are denoted by a little figure 1, 2 or 3 written just after and just above the whole number; so 15³ means 15¾ft². If you're buying skins you'll probably have to buy whole skins, anything from 5 to 10ft² on average. If hide is what you want, and you don't need whole hides or sides, try for shoulders, backs, bellies, etc. The firmest, best-quality leather comes from the back and shoulders. Other cowhide leathers come in the areas mentioned on page 12.

The 'substance' or thickness of leather is, very sensibly, measured in millimetres. Different thicknesses have different general uses:

Use	Substance in mm
Linings, gloves, trimmings	0·4 –1·0
Garments, gloves, purses	1·0 –1·5
Upholstery, handbags, shoe uppers	1·25–2·0
Medium/heavy duty luggage, belts, saddlery	1·75–3·0
Tooling and carving, belts, unsupported seating	3·0 –5·0
Soles, machinery casings	5·0 –8·0 and over

Sole leather is sold differently. You buy it by the pound weight, so much per pound. The thickness of sole leather is measured in irons, 1 iron equals ¼₈in; therefore 12 iron leather is ¼in or 6·5mm thick. Sandal soles need to be in the 10–12 iron range, that is between ⅕ and ¼in, or between 5·5 and 6·5mm thick. Leather this thick weighs somewhere between 14oz and 18oz per square foot.

Prices

The price of leather has everything to do with quality and durability, and, especially where hide is concerned, with thickness. Every type of leather has its own price range, sometimes fairly wide, depending on its quality and the place you buy it from. At the time of writing 'cheap' meant 40–50p per square foot and 'expensive' £1·50 or more per square foot. Here is a very approximate league table of the leathers mentioned on pages 14–17.

Cheap

skiver, belly hide, cowhide splits

chamois, garment cowhide

thin hide (up to 1·5mm), Niger goat, nappa, cabretta, sueded kip, pig suede

medium hide (up to 2·5mm), upholstery cowhide, full kip, suede calf

thick hide (up to 4mm), thin latigo, cape, Morocco, doeskin

sole leather, thick latigo, calf, kid, pigskin,
Expensive peccary, hogskin

Always buy the best quality you can afford, especially if you are buying suede splits or hide for dyeing and tooling. Really good work can be spoiled by inferior leather.

Where to buy

General craft shops, leather retailers, wholesale leather merchants, tanners – they all sell leather. Here are the main pros and cons in our experience:

General craft shops	Leather retailers	Wholesale leather merchants	Tanners
Sell scraps and part skins, sometimes belt lengths and kits	Sell scraps, kits, belt lengths, whole and half hides, sometimes part hides and usually only whole skins	Sell whole and half hides, also backs, shoulders, bends, etc. according to their speciality, whole skins only	Sell whole skins only, also whole and half hides, sometimes backs, shoulders, bends, etc. according to their speciality
Choice very limited	Good choice of type and colour	Good choice within speciality	Fair choice within speciality
Expensive	Expensive	Reasonable price	Very good value for money

With these points in mind, how do you find out where to buy?

Look first in your local Yellow Pages or trade directory under 'leather merchants', 'leather dressers and finishers', 'leather manufacturers', 'tanners', 'hide and skin merchants'. Ring up the nearest and find out what they specialize in and whether they sell small quantities.

Trade associations are invaluable sources of information. Your local library will have the name and address of your national or regional leather association. In the UK it is the Leather Institute (address in Appendix). Write to them for a list of small quantity suppliers.

Most of the suppliers listed in the Appendix will supply

leather by post, but write for catalogues first. Buying in person is a lot more interesting of course. That way you'll get nearer to what you want. You'll also learn more than any book can tell you.

How to buy

It would be very easy to say 'never buy until you know exactly what you want to make, the size of it as well as the design'. But it doesn't always work like that. It's a question of bringing together two things, your idea and your material. Visualize your design as clearly as possible but be ready to compromise on your leather, especially on colour. Thickness and consistency are more important than getting the exact shade. If you do have a pattern, take it with you when you buy.

Assuming you are inside your first leather warehouse and know roughly what you want, ask where the tooling hide or nappa or garment cowhide is and have a quiet look around. Can you see just what you are looking for? Probably not. Take your time. Would something else do? If no brilliant solution occurs to you after a good twenty minutes, ask for a small sample of the possibles and leave. Don't start asking questions and prices until you've seen two or three possibles and don't pretend you know more than you do.

Another approach, guileless this one, is simply to say 'I want to make a so and so. What sort of leather would you suggest?' Most warehousemen react well to being asked for advice.

You'll probably have a choice of skins/hides of the type you finally choose. Don't be fobbed off with the top one in the pile, but be reasonable. Every skin has a blemish or two. Usually one can arrange to cut round marks or holes. Generally speaking the larger the skin the greater the proportion of usable to total area. Choose a nice firm skin, one that doesn't stretch too readily. If you want to buy in quantity, ask for a discount.

Storing leather

Keep hide flat rather than rolled up. Grain leathers can be rolled up, grain side outwards, with brown paper. Splits are best kept flat. Always let leather breathe, in other words don't enclose it in polythene. Heat and sunlight cause leather to dry out and darken.

Cleaning leather

Hide and smooth grain leathers can be cleaned and conditioned with saddle soap. Work the soap into a lather with water and sponge it evenly onto the leather. Wipe off the excess with a dry cloth, and when dry buff to restore the shine. Ordinary mild soap and water lifts grease and dirt from chrome tanned leather quite effectively, but without conditioning it like saddle soap.

Good haberdashery departments stock a range of leather cleaners, usually the spray-on sort, for glossy grain leathers, matt grain leathers and suede. Read the instructions carefully and always experiment on a sample first. Steer clear of small bottles of dry cleaning fluid – they contain solvents which may remove the dye.

Dirt marks on suede can sometimes be teased off with a stiff bristle brush, very fine glasspaper or an art rubber (the cheesy sort). You can also buy small pumice blocks for erasing marks on suede.

When the time comes for total cleaning of an article, as opposed to removing the odd grease or dirt spot, take it to a specialist cleaner. He will assess whether it should be dry cleaned or wet cleaned; he knows how cleaning solvents react to dyes – he's probably spent years becoming a proficient leather cleaner – and how to re-tint, re-oil and re-finish an article after cleaning.

Don't be tempted to wash leather garments, even chamois or buckskin. Ten to one they'll lose their shape and softness.

Conditioning leather

Saddle soap, liberally applied with the fingers, is the best all-purpose conditioner for hide and all smooth grain leathers. Wipe off the excess and get out the elbow grease. If your leather still has a sticky feel after a few minutes of rubbing, go on rubbing.

Neatsfoot oil, 'hide food' and 'leather food' (even mink oil!), can all be used to lubricate and soften smooth grain leather. Water resistant finishes for grain leathers include saddle soap, neatsfoot oil, dubbin (a mixture of oil and tallow which gives a matt finish), various commercially available lacquers, cover coats and scuff coats, and, of course, polish. Castor oil gives a lovely shine. So do neutral cream shoe polishes.

Flattening soft leathers

For accurate pattern cutting you need flat leather. Try making wrinkles and creases disappear by pulling and stretching. If you're the patient type weight your leather down on a flat surface with lots of heavy books. If you want quicker results, though, you'll have to resort to ironing. Always use a cool, dry iron, never place it directly on the leather (put a sheet of brown paper between the iron and the leather) and keep the iron moving. A hot iron, or leaning hard on a stationary iron, will give you an everlasting set of wrinkles like the wrinkles on the sand when the tide is out.

2 Tools and equipment

What follows is not an exhaustive list of leatherworking gear. On the other hand it covers all the basic tools and other sundries needed to cope with everything we talk about in this book. But don't wilt and despair as you read on – you don't have to dash out and buy the lot, maybe not even a quarter of it. We've got to get the information down somewhere and it's difficult to give a list of absolute musts because it depends entirely on what you choose to make. For this reason we give a list of 'Tools and equipment' needed under each article described in the second part of the book. So peruse these lists first, then turn back to this chapter to find out what we're talking about, and just accumulate things as you need them. Anyway, here's what you might need later if not sooner, or perhaps not at all. Many of the tools we talk about are photographed on the back cover. (See Appendix for a list of suppliers.)

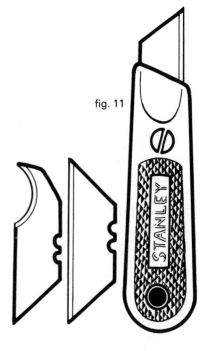

fig. 11

Working surface

A sturdy table is best. Cover it with a sheet of hardboard to protect the top. You can cut directly on this or better still on a piece of plywood. This won't blunt your knives so quickly.

Cutting tools

Stanley knife and steel rule There are special leather knives for cutting cowhide but we find a Stanley knife plus two types of blade, one straight, one curved (figure 11), does everything needed and at half the price. For cutting straight lines in hide or other thick leather use the Stanley with its normal straight blade against a steel rule. A 12in rule is fine. Hold it down firmly on the leather. There's no necessity to complete the cut in one go, keep going over it until you're through.

To cut curves, fix the curved blade in the Stanley. This is the type recommended for lino cutting and it slices through leather a treat. There are two methods of negotiating a curve. One way is to make a shallow cut first, following the

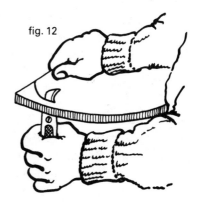

fig. 12

pattern line pencilled on the leather, then go over and over the cut as before. If you're using a cardboard pattern you can make the initial cut against the edge of it.

The second method may sound a bit alarming, but it does result in a good clean cut, hopefully in the leather! Practise cutting up some scrap leather to get the hang of it and work with a really sharp blade, but only try this on reasonably stiff hide. Hold the leather horizontal in one hand and using the Stanley upright, pare towards you through the leather following the pattern line carefully (figure 12). Keep control of the knife and avoid fingers and jugular. Unless you have exceptionally strong hands and nerves you'll never get through sole leather this way. (See page 117 for cutting sandal soles.)

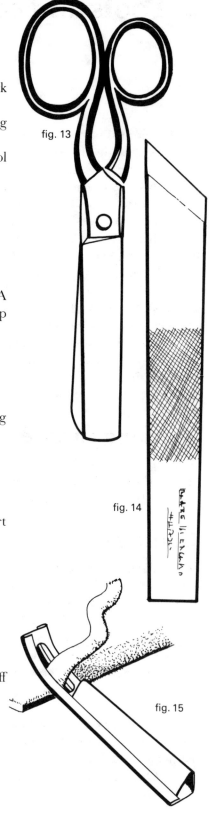

fig. 13

fig. 14

fig. 15

Leather shears These are first class for snipping through anything from skiver to hide, especially heavyweight garment leather (but they won't get through sole leather). A robust pair of dressmaking scissors can cope with leather up to about 1·5mm thick but this blunts them quickly. Really it's your choice – shears are reasonably expensive but a good investment (figure 13).

Scissors A small pair of sharp scissors are invaluable for appliqué work (page 65), trimming thin leather and cutting laces (page 39).

Skiving knife You often need to reduce the thickness of leather to make joins, overlaps or folds less bulky. This is called 'skiving' and it's done with a skiving knife on the wrong (usually the flesh) side of the leather. We use the sort in figure 14. There are other types which work just as well so don't worry if the ones in your shop aren't exactly the same. Make sure the blade is razor sharp before you start skiving (see Appendix, page 137, for sharpening hints). You skive like this. Lay your leather on anything hard and smooth. A piece of plate glass, a slab of marble or a flat metal surface is fine, but failing these hardboard will do. Hold the knife at a low angle and work away from yourself with short oblique strokes. Keep at it until you've shaved off an even amount all along the edge.

Safety skiver (figure 15) This is another skiving tool. It takes replaceable blades and is designed to prevent you gouging right through the leather. We find it works well on most edges and is good for skiving in the middle of leather.

Any DIY or tool shop should have a Stanley knife. Look there too or in a good stationers for a steel rule. You may track down leather shears and skiving knives in some craft shops, otherwise try your nearest leather tools supplier.

Hammering

Hammer (figure 16) You need an ordinary steel hammer for setting rivets, eyelets and press studs – any tool shop should have one. Never use this type of flat-faced hammer directly on leather because it will leave edge marks. (You can buy special round-faced steel leatherwork hammers that won't leave marks, but we find a mallet's a good substitute and more useful all round.)

Mallet Leatherwork can involve a fair amount of pounding and whacking, especially if you are making footwear. Other times you may want to flatten and reduce the bulk of a seam or set a glued join. A mallet is the tool for the job. It's also handy for using with punches, stamping or carving tools. You'll probably meet two types, wood and rawhide (figure 17). Either sort in a medium weight is fine for most tasks. It's a good idea to round the edge on one end with a file and use that end for thumping leather and the other for hitting punches and stamps. If you can't locate one in a craft shop you might try a tool shop for the wooden sort, otherwise it's back to a leather tools supplier.

Wooden block Do all your stamping and punching on a solid base. A chunk of tree trunk is ideal, alternatively use a thick piece of wood on a stout table. (Do all your hammering over one of the legs to reduce vibration, and noise.)

Last We really only mention this as a possible acquisition. If you want to make dozens of sandals then it's worthwhile looking around for one simply because it's much easier to keep straps and things out of the way if you're pounding your soles on something foot-shaped. Your best bet is to go along to your local cobbler and ask where he gets his hardware from. But for the one-off pair of sandals a flat metal anvil, the top of a metal vice, really any hefty piece of metal you can lay your hands on will do. If you've none of these, resort to a tree stump or figure 19 shows the type of last we found in the garden shed!

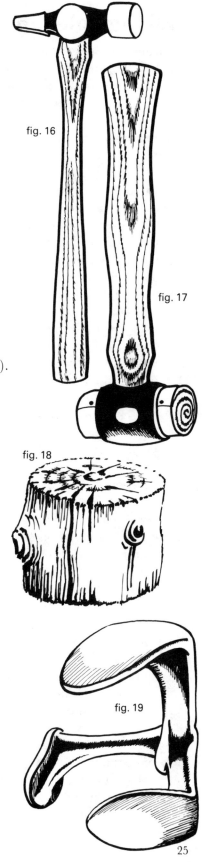

fig. 16

fig. 17

fig. 18

fig. 19

Making holes and slits

Just a general word. Whether you're using drive or slit punches, thonging chisels or awls, and this goes for metal stamping tools too, hit them with a mallet and not a steel hammer.

Rotary punch (figure 20) This is a must. The head carries six different size punches with which to make holes in straps and belts, and holes for rivets or eyelets. This punch will get through most leathers except very tough hide and sole leather. For this you'll have to use a drive punch. In fact if you've got literally hundreds of holes to punch a drive punch is easier on the wrist.

Don't forget that you can use the rotary punch to make holes in the middle of leather. Select the size punch needed and position it opposite, not against, the anvil or pad. Place this punch on the leather and holding the handles together hit the anvil with the mallet. In the long run it probably doesn't do the punch much good but for the odd few holes it's very handy. (See figure 21.)

DIY or tool shops plus some haberdashery departments should be able to produce a rotary punch. It doesn't pay to go for the cheapest. Check that all the punches meet the anvil squarely and click into place firmly. (For sharpening see Appendix, page 137.)

Drive punches The commonest types of drive punch are round ones for making holes (the large type are sometimes called wad punches) and oblong ones (bag or crew punches) for making slots (figure 22). You may need a slot for attaching a buckle (see page 54), making a bag fastening or attaching sandal straps. Both types of punch can be bought singly in a range of sizes or in sets which combine some circular and some oblong. The larger the punch the more expensive it is so wait and see what you really need. Work on your tree stump or wooden block, grasp the punch firmly and hit it squarely with the mallet. If you've just got one slot to cut and it's not likely to be too conspicuous there's no need to lash out on a separate punch. You can cut it quite neatly as shown in figure 88 on page 54.

Slit punches (figure 23a) You may need these to make slits for lacing or to take the flat prongs of a metal fastening. They range in width from about 2 to 6mm. You can manage with a Stanley knife if you've just got a couple of slits to

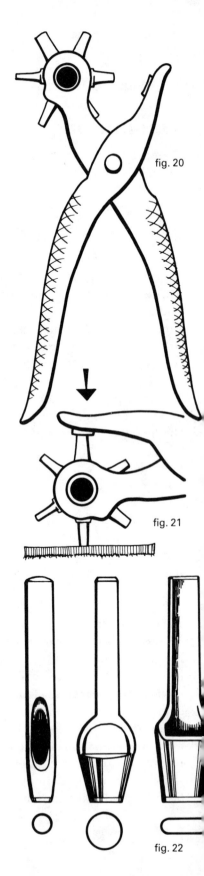

fig. 20

fig. 21

fig. 22

make. Incidentally, if you already have a small wooden chisel, that's one size slit punch you needn't buy.

Thonging chisels These are just like small forks on which the prongs (anything from three to eight in number) are mini slit punches. They're very time-saving for punching rows and rows of lacing slits. Incidentally the very small-pronged ones are good for making stitch holes. On some the prongs are aligned (figure 23c), on others they're twisted to give parallel slits (figure 23b). The few-pronged punches are best for negotiating curves. Hit them with the mallet and to keep the spacing between sets of slits constant, insert an end prong in the last slit made.

Awls These are mainly used for making stitch holes. There are two common varieties, a round awl (figure 24a), and a harness awl (figure 24b) which has a diamond-shaped blade. To make holes with the round awl just tap it gently with the mallet. Occasionally you may need to make stitch holes in an assembled item where it's impossible to use the mallet and round awl. In these cases stab away with the harness awl.

Hand stitching

Stitchmarker (figure 25a) This tool makes accurate guide marks for punching stitch holes – you just run the wheel along your stitch line. The teeth on the wheel are equally spaced to give a certain number of stitch marks to the inch. In theory this means you need a different stitchmarker for each different length stitch you use, but in practice you need only use every second or third mark. Therefore the more teeth to the inch, the greater your options. Ones which mark 8 or 10 stitches to the inch are the most common. When you buy check that the wheel runs smoothly. Although stitchmarkers are always recommended as a basic tool, we have got by in the past just measuring and marking the holes with a ruler and sharp pencil or awl. If your budget is really tight this is one tool you could do without. NB. Stitchmarkers don't make much impression on suede so it's best to measure and mark this with fine biro on the wrong side.

Sewing needles There are two sorts traditionally used for leatherwork. One has a sharp triangular point which pierces soft leather easily and can be used without pre-

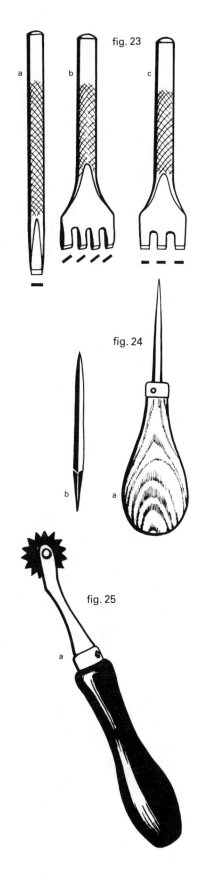

fig. 23

fig. 24

fig. 25

punched holes on thin and medium weight leather. We call this a *leather needle* (figure 25c). Its other name is a glover's needle. Remember that this type can't be used for saddle stitching or backstitching (page 37) because its cutting point will sever the previous stitch.

The other sort is the *harness needle* (sometimes called a saddler's needle) and this is the one you're most likely to use (figure 25b). It's a strong needle with an egg-shaped eye and blunt end. You use it for stitching through pre-punched holes in all weights of leather. You'll mostly need it for saddle stitching, which is a two-needle technique, so buy the needles in pairs. In emergency we've made our own harness needles by blunting ordinary sewing ones on a sharpening block or emery paper.

Leather and harness needles come in different sizes so just choose ones to suit the thickness of your thread and the weight of the leather (see comments on page 36).

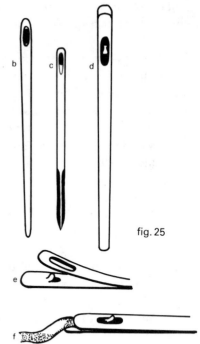

fig. 25

Lacing needle (figure 25d) These are large flat needles with heads that split in two (figures 25e, f). One half of the head has a little prong that's supposed to pierce the end of the lace and hold it firmly sandwiched in the head of the needle. In fact it's best to stab a tiny hole in the lace end first, then prise open and wedge the needle head apart with your fingernails while you get the lace fixed over the prong. In theory this sounds fine, in practice it's a little fiddly, but once it's all strung up it does make light work of intricate lacing.

Actually if you're lacing through pre-punched holes, it's often as easy to cut the end of the lace to a point, stiffen it with glue, then just poke it through the holes. If you're working through reasonably large slits you can prod the lace through quite well with a harness needle or awl. (See page 39 for other remarks about lacing with a needle.)

Thimble Handstitching can be tough on the fingers so get yourself a thimble.

Stitching awl (figure 26) This is handy if you're stitching in awkward corners or through thick leather where it's difficult to manipulate two harness needles. It does a lock stitch, rather like a sewing machine. We won't explain how it works here because it will come with clear instructions. It does have a point for stabbing through leather but it's best to use pre-punched holes just to make the work easier and neater. Other comments about using stitching awls appear on pages 36 and 37. There's no point in buying one till you think you really need one.

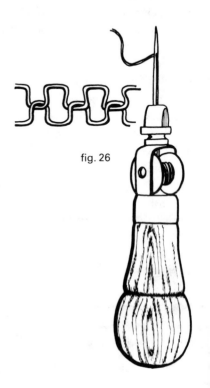

fig. 26

28

Thread Use button thread or Sylko 40 for fine stitching on thin leathers, otherwise use a waxed linen thread – waxed because it helps prevent the thread from rotting and stops it fraying as it's pulled through the holes, and linen because this is stronger than cotton. Special waxed 3-strand linen thread is kept by most leathercraft suppliers. They're almost bound to have black, cream and brown or tan. Occasionally they stock other colours too. More hints on threads appear on page 36.

Pliers A pair of ordinary pliers are good for pulling needles through tight holes.

Machine stitching

The pros and cons of machine stitching are covered on page 38. Really, a sewing machine is only practical on thin leather.

Edging tools

Edge beveller (figure 27a) This is a good investment. It's used to bevel raw hide edges and give them a more finished look, so it's especially useful on belts and bags. (Remember to do all your bevelling before you dye the leather.) There are different sizes of beveller – they just take off more or less of the edge (figure 27b). A medium size is the most useful.

Edge groover (figure 28a) This is used for making a groove parallel and close to an edge, usually for finishing purposes, or to take recessed stitching. The edge groover is an odd-looking beast so here's how you use it. Set the main prong or heel against the edge of the leather and pull towards you. As you do so the round eye on the little cross-arm cuts a neat U-shaped groove (figure 28b). A screw in the end of the main prong allows the cross-arm to be moved so you can alter the distance of the eye from the edge.
It's not limited to an edging tool either. If you angle it a bit you can use it to cut grooves in the middle of leather. Use it freehand or against a hard edge (like a steel rule, saucer edge or even a coin) for decorative grooves on the grain side, or for making fold-line grooves on the flesh side.
There are adjustable V-shaped groovers, sometimes called gouges, on the market but these are push tools and on balance we find the above type more versatile and easier to use. The V-shaped groover is an advantage if you're

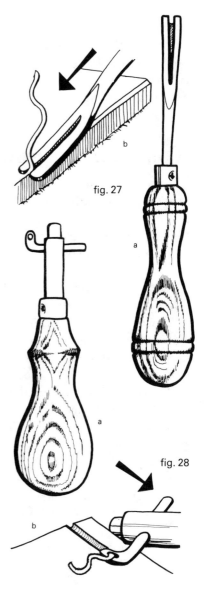

fig. 27

fig. 28

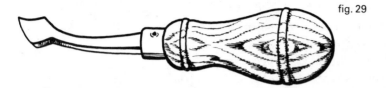

fig. 29

working with really thick leather and need deep grooves to
achieve a good right-angle bend or to take stitching in a
recessed seam.

Edge creaser (figure 29) This impresses grooves along edges
and can be used on hide or softer leather. It's simply an
extra finishing tool and one you can probably do without.
Actually you get a similar effect using the back of a knife
against a steel rule.

Burnisher (figure 30) This is a must for finishing hide edges.
It's a smooth plastic (sometimes hardwood) wheel with a
groove round the rim. Fit it over the edge of the leather and
rub hard till you get a smooth, shiny finish. On sole edges
anything hard and smooth – a milk bottle, the back of a
spoon – will serve as a burnisher.

fig. 30

Tools for designing on leather

fig. 31

Stamps There are dozens of different metal stamps
available from leathercraft suppliers. (In catalogues these
are also referred to as fancy punches or dies.) They range
from simple geometric ones (figure 31) to quite complex
motif stamps that you can use singly or to make a panel of
repeated pattern. Hit them with the mallet and work on
leather dampened with water. Dampening the leather, back
and front, makes it receptive to imprints which will then be
held when the leather dries.

You can make your own simple stamps using small lengths
of hardwood moulding. This can usually be bought in small
square, semi-circular, oblong and quadrant section. If these
still prove too large, cut smaller or different shapes in the
end of a piece (figure 32). Use a coping saw to do this and
sand the end of the wood smooth. These stamps should last
pretty well for a good few dozen imprints; then the edges
lose their sharpness. On the other hand a screw or bolt fixed
into the end of a piece of hardwood (figure 32) will give
endless clear imprints. We used this method to make the
pattern on the Carrying Straps, page 51.

Carving tools These are discussed in Chapter 8.

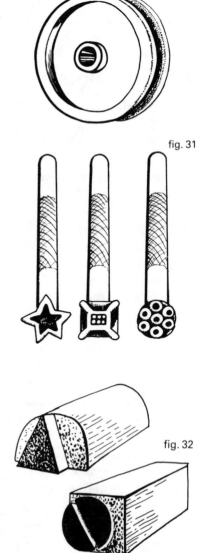

fig. 32

Groovers We've already mentioned under 'Edging tools' that you can use the edge groover for freehand line designs. Just for the sake of completeness we ought to say that you can buy a plain simple groover (figure 33a) and various types of race, e.g. figure 33b. Both of these cut grooves when pulled across the leather either freehand or against a hard edge.

Soldering iron Details of the type of iron to use for burning designs on leather are given on page 89.

Rivets, eyelets and press studs

Here we'll just cover these three standard metal fastenings. Other hardware is mentioned in Chapter 6 on fastenings, page 53. Good haberdashery departments often stock packets of rivets, eyelets and press studs. They all require setting tools and these are either packaged with the fastenings themselves or should be available separately. If they're separate, double check that you're buying the right tools for the type and size of fastening.

Setting tools usually comprise a little metal anvil and a metal punch that you hit with your steel hammer (see figure 34a). Some of the tools are specific to the size of fastening, so for example if you want to use two sizes of eyelets you'll have to pay out for two lots of setting tools.

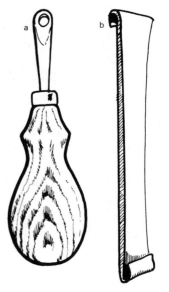

fig. 33

Rivets These are used as an alternative to joining by stitching or lacing. There are two types, split and tubular. We prefer tubular rivets (figure 34b) because they make a neat finish back and front. They come in two parts, head and base. The hole in your leather should fit the shank of the head. When you press the two parts of the rivet together through the leather they should just click together. Then you just place the base on the anvil, put the punch on the head and hit it smartly with the hammer a few times. Work on a firm surface, e.g. your tree stump or block of wood. Before buying check you've got the right length rivet – roughly the same length as the combined thicknesses of the leather you're joining. If they're too short the two parts will never hold together, if too long the head will deform when you set the rivet and the join will be loose. Should things go awry and you need to remove a rivet try to buckle the flange on the base with a screwdriver or chisel so you can pull it through the leather. It's best not to try levering the head off, because it doesn't always work and you risk damaging the good side of the leather.

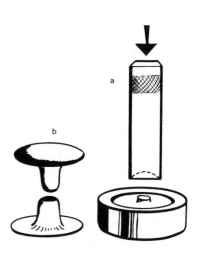

fig. 34

Eyelets (figure 35) Use these to finish lacing, belt and strap holes (make sure they're big enough to take the buckle prong) or simply as decoration. They come in two hole sizes usually and they're very easy to set.

You may have seen really huge eyelets on bought bags and things. We've seen these referred to as 'sail' eyelets. Unlike small eyelets they come in two parts and are set rather like a rivet. Not every leathercraft supplier seems to have them so you may have to shop around.

Press studs or snap fastenings These make strong fastenings for wristbands, bags and clothes. You can get them in different sizes with all sorts of decorative heads. They come in four parts, a, b, c and d which go together in two pairs as shown in figure 36, usually packaged with details on which part goes with what. If you buy them loose check carefully that you've got a correct set.

Other things

Glue You're bound to need glue sooner or later. For all lighter jobs like turning and gluing hems, lining belts, holding leather together prior to stitching, etc. we find UHU or Bostic 1 Clear Adhesive works well. Both dry clear and give strong flexible bonds insoluble in water or dry cleaning solvents. Careful how you spread them, they're difficult to remove from the wrong place. For heavier jobs like gluing sandal soles, or for that matter whenever you need to glue layers of hide together we would recommend Phillips Neoprene adhesive. This dries to make a wellnigh immovable bond and can be sanded with the leather edge – other glues tend to pull out.

Follow instructions for use carefully and if you are working on a smooth grain surface roughen it to provide a good key for the glue. In fact you can buy a special tool (called a ruffer) for doing this but actually a wire brush or coarse glasspaper will do. On soling leather you may actually have to score the leather lightly all over.

Sanding block If you've glued together several layers of stiff hide, say for handles or sandals, or moulded something in thick sole leather (page 84), you may need to sand the edge smooth. Do this with a simple sanding block made by wrapping a piece of fine glasspaper tightly round a little block of wood (wrap it round a thick piece of dowel for curved surfaces). The edge will go fuzzy; to smooth it

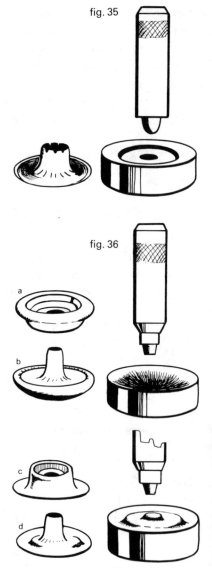

fig. 35

fig. 36

a

b

c

d

dampen with a wet sponge then burnish with something smooth and hard. (A power drill speeds up the process no end, see page 118.)

Saddle soap This is excellent stuff and we can't recommend it enough. It imparts a smooth natural sheen to grain leather (not suede). There are products around which claim to give all kinds of wonderful gloss or lacquer finishes to leather, but for our money we'd rather stick to good old saddle soap. It helps to soften and clean leather, gives it a water resistant finish, is safe to use on dyed or untreated leather, and you can often get it in shoe shops, sports shops or hardware stores. Put it on with a non-fluff cloth or your fingers and rub well to bring up a shine.

Neatsfoot oil This is a natural oil obtained from the feet of oxen ('neat' means a bovine). It keeps leather supple by preventing it from drying out and cracking, so it's good for sandals, which take a lot of bending. Rub it on liberally – you'll find raw leather will absorb masses. Neatsfoot will darken the leather slightly. Finish off with saddle soap if you like.

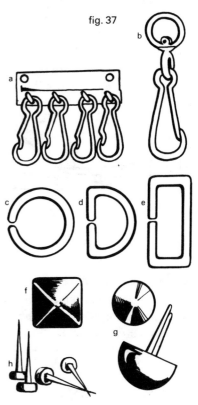

fig. 37

Beeswax Pure beeswax can be bought in little cakes from some hardware shops and chemists, plus, of course, from leathercraft suppliers. Use it for sealing and polishing hide edges. Rub it on before you get to work with the burnisher.

Dyes These and other colouring methods are given a chapter of their own, page 45.

Miscellaneous hardware All fastenings to do with belts and bags are gone into in Chapter 6 and rivets, eyelets and press studs have their own section in this chapter. Here we'll just mention the odd few things you might require, all of which should be available from a leathercraft supplier and some of them from a good craft shop.
Figure 37 shows key case fitting (a); leash clip (b); metal ring, D-ring and rectangle (c, d, e); dog collar studs (f); and dome stud (g) for protecting the bottom of bags. We've also shown cobbling nails (h) – for use and availability of these see page 118.

3 Joining

There are four ways of joining leather: gluing, stitching, lacing or thonging, and riveting. Some articles, garments for example, are a clearcut case for stitching. Others stay together just as well with lacing or riveting. Joining is a structural operation, but it can be decorative too.

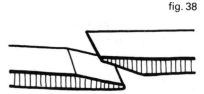

fig. 38

Preparing a join

Joins can be made less bulky by skiving the edges or areas concerned. You'll need a safety skiver or skiving knife to do this. Take joining lengths of strap or lacing: both ends can be skived so that there is no noticeable increase in thickness at the join (figure 38).

Skiving along one, both or all of the edges involved in a join also makes the join more flexible and in some cases easier to stitch (figure 39a, b, c, d).

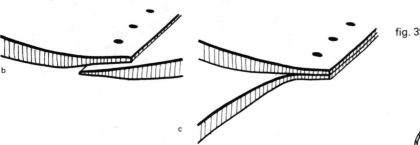

fig. 39

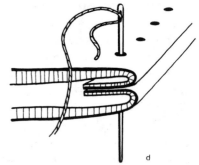

Skiving tools need to be very sharp for paring splits. Hide and grain leathers skive rather better. Usually, though not always, skiving is done on the flesh side.

Some surfaces, sandal soles for example, need roughening up with glasspaper or a fierce wire brush before gluing.

Types of join

Most major joins are 'seams', in the sense that they involve joining smaller pieces of leather together to make larger pieces or shapes. The most useful types of seam for joining leather are the plain seam, the overlap seam and the abutted seam.

Plain seams These can be stitched, laced or riveted with the wrong sides of the leather together, or, if you're working with thin leather, stitched with right sides together and turned right sides out at a later stage. On thin leather a plain seam can be pressed open in various ways (figure 40a, b, c) with the aid of glue and a mallet, and emphasized with topstitching or lacing.

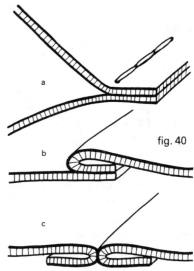

fig. 40

Overlap and abutted seams (figure 41) These can also be joined by stitching, lacing or riveting – the thickness of the leather and the function of the article being made usually dictate which method is the most suitable. Abutted seams are often backed (figure 42a) with a strip of leather or cotton tape; glue the backing strip to one edge first, then butt the second edge against the first. Skip the backing if you decide to stitch or lace to and fro across the join (figure 42b).

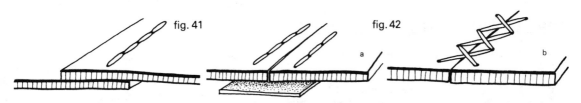

fig. 41   fig. 42

Recessed seams (figure 43) These are primarily a feature of soles (see comments on Moccasins, page 112). Here the stitching sits in a specially cut groove to prevent it rubbing and fraying – very useful on some hide bags and belts too. An edge groover is the tool you need here.

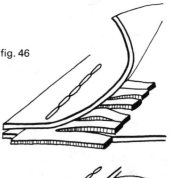

fig. 43

Piped and fringed seams (figures 44–47) Piping, with or without piping cord inside it, can be sandwiched into a plain or overlap seam for extra emphasis. So can strips of fringe. Conventionally, piped or fringed seams are stitched (the Pouffe on page 49 has piped plain seams top and bottom), but there could be occasions when lacing or riveting would be functional.

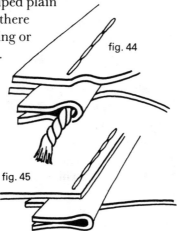

fig. 44

fig. 45

fig. 46

fig. 47

As we have said, most joins fall into the seam category. Other types of join involve attaching small items – straps, handles, pockets, loops – to the back or front of larger pieces of leather. Attachment in such cases can be by stitching, riveting or lacing.

Gluing

We have already mentioned gluing in connection with soles. Glue is adequate for bonding soles to topsoles (see page 118) or for sticking two or more thicknesses of leather together for use as a single thickness (see Moccasins, page 112). But it's not satisfactory for the general run of joins except for holding them together while you make a permanent join in the form of lacing, stitching or riveting. You'll find comments on glue on page 32.

Hand stitching

Needles and thread As you will have gathered from page 27 you have a choice of weapons for hand stitching: leather needle, harness needle or stitching awl. And a choice of threads. Stitching awls work best with thickish thread and thickish leather. Though they're usually sold complete with a bobbin of waxed linen thread, there's nothing to stop you winding some different strong thread onto the bobbin.
If you want nice conspicuous stitching, work with waxed 3-strand linen thread, unwaxed 3-strand linen thread, button thread – very strong all of these – or any of the threads sold as 'topstitching' threads. Sylko 40, usually described as 'suitable for medium/heavyweight natural fabrics' is strong enough for most garment seams, but it's much finer. If a thread frays or fuzzes as you pull it through your leather, it's no good.
Thin needles go with thin thread and thin leather, thick ones with thick thread and thick leather – common sense really.

Making stitch holes For most jobs involving harness or leather needles or a stitching awl you'll find you need to make your stitch holes with a round awl and mallet first, or with a harness awl as you go along. Only on the thinnest leather can you pierce and stitch in one operation. Always glue, sellotape or paperclip joins before you start stitching or making holes.
Use a stitchmarker, or a ruler and a marker (the point of a

round awl on grain leather, pencil on hide, biro on suede) to get your holes evenly spaced. Your stitches can afford to be pretty big, up to 6mm (¼in), say, on thick leather, but don't go to the other extreme with thin leather. Too many stitch holes and your leather might tear along the seam. NB. You can use a sewing machine, unthreaded but fitted with a leather needle, to make rows of stitch holes on thin grain leather.

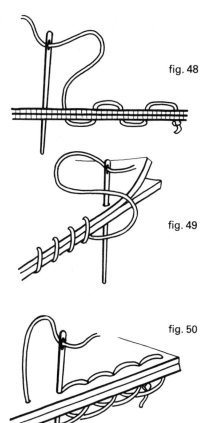

fig. 48

fig. 49

fig. 50

Types of stitch If you are using a leather needle, which probably means you are working with thin leather, your choice of stitches is limited to running stitch (figure 48) and overcast stitch (figure 49), neither of which involves poking the needle twice through the same stitch hole.

Back stitch (figure 50) and saddle stitch (figure 51) make stronger joins than running or overcast stitch. This is where you need harness needles, two in the case of saddle stitch, and pre-pierced holes. Just try back or saddle stitch with a leather needle and you'll see why harness needles were invented. You don't actually poke both needles through the hole at the same time!

Any of the following stitches make strong structural seams as well as decorative topstitching: zigzag, cross, herringbone and blanket (figures 52–54). Cross and herringbone could be done with a leather needle.

Only one type of stitch, a lock stitch, is possible with a stitching awl (see figure 55). Whether you look at it from the back or the front it is indistinguishable from saddle stitch.

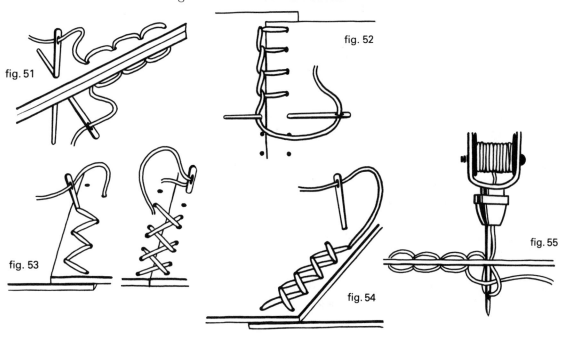

fig. 52

fig. 51

fig. 53

fig. 54

fig. 55

Machine stitching

First, machine stitching is only feasible on thin leather.
Second, you need special leather needles; medium thickness
ones are best because they stab through the leather without
too much resistance but have an eye with a groove deep
enough to take the thread through the leather without
fraying it. Third, Sylko 40 is the thread to use. Button
thread is too thick to struggle round the bobbin mechanism
and make the lock stitch properly.

There's a lot of friction between the needle and the leather,
and between the thread and the leather, so stitch fairly
slowly. If you have 'feeding' problems, i.e. the grain side of
the leather slips against the teeth of the feed dog, put some
tissue paper between the leather and the foot plate. Try
medium tension top and bottom to start with, and medium
foot pressure. Missed or unlocked stitches may be due to an
accumulation of greasy lint around the bobbin mechanism.
Poke around with a stiff hair brush until the mechanism is
clean and start again.

Experiment with double, treble and quadruple thickness
scraps first. This will enable you to assess how much of the
article you are making can be sewn by machine, and how
much skiving you need to do to reduce bulk in seams.
Glue, paper clip or sellotape seams before you stitch.
Running stitch or zigzag are probably your only options (we
used zigzag across the abutted edges of the seams on the
Tunic, page 74.). Don't make your stitches too tiny.
At the risk of sounding dismal, hand stitching is sometimes
quicker and produces better-looking results than machine
stitching, especially on medium and thick leathers.

Lacing

Everything joinable with thread can be joined in almost
exactly the same way with lacing. In other words it is
possible to duplicate any of the seams and stitches
illustrated on page 37 with lacing. The Bolster photographed
on page 74, for example, has overlap seams 'sewn' with
zigzag style lacing. The Carpet Bag on page 51 has side seams
'sewn' with saddle stitch style lacing. Many other
combinations are equally robust and decorative (see
'Laced hide edges', page 42).

Buying versus cutting laces 'Lacing' in this context
means round or square hide thonging as well as the flat sort

cut from thinnish grain leather. Craft stores sell thonging and lacing in pre-cut lengths or by the metre. The flat sort come in various colours, widths and thicknesses.

Cutting your own lacing is much cheaper of course. Sharp scissors or a Stanley knife and a steel rule are the obvious tools for the job, but longer lengths of lacing can sometimes be got out of smaller pieces of leather by the spiral cutting method (figure 56). For this you need a small, sharp pair of scissors and a steady hand. Cut a circle of leather first, then cut in from the edge in a spiral, keeping the width of the lacing as constant as possible. Until you're confident, mark guide cutting lines in biro on the back of your leather. It stands to reason that stretchy leather is more suitable for spiral-cut lacing than firm leather, because it's easier to pull straight. Naturally the smaller the circle you start with the more twisty the lacing will be.

fig. 56

Lacing cut from splits is weaker than grain lacing, but useful for purely decorative purposes.

Joining lacing Lengths of flat lacing should be joined by skiving and gluing the ends (see figure 38 on page 34). Glue lengths together as you go along rather than getting into a ravel with very long pre-joined lengths. Make any joins on the back of your work.

Making holes and slits Lacing holes are made with a rotary or drive punch, and slits with a slit punch or multiple-pronged thonging chisel. Glue, clip or sellotape your joins before you make holes or slits, or if this is impracticable make separate matching sets of slits or holes in the sections to be joined. For really snug joins your holes and slits should be very slightly smaller than your thonging or lacing. In our opinion lacing through holes is structurally stronger than lacing through slits and it's often a lot easier. (The Bolster on page 74 and the Carpet Bag on page 51 were each laced together through holes.) Round or square thonging looks best threaded through holes too.

Holes reinforced with eyelets are a good idea, not only for extra strength but to make joins easy to lace and unlace.

Threading There are special lacing needles for threading flat lacing (see page 28). If the lacing keeps slipping out of the eye wrap a small piece of sellotape round the eye and the lace. Make sure the same side of the lace, usually the grain side, shows on every 'stitch' – you may have to twist the lace on the back of your work.

Hide and rawhide lacing have ends stiff enough to poke through holes and slits, but you can speed things up by gluing and pinching the ends hard, or stiffening them with sellotape.

Most laced joins benefit from flattening with a mallet.

Riveting

Rivets are commonly used to attach buckles to straps, straps to bags, etc. (see page 99) but they can also be used, sometimes very decoratively, on thick leather where sewn or laced edges look too genteel (figure 57). Eyelets could be used for the same purpose. You'll need the correct setting tools for the size of rivet or eyelet and a rotary or drive punch to make the holes. Punch one set of holes, then draw through them to mark the exact position of the second set. Hold your leather together with paper clips, glue or sellotape while you do this.

fig. 57

4 Edges

Edges get noticed. Almost more than anything else they mark you down as a craftsman . . . or a botcher! Often a well-finished edge is all the decoration an article requires. Care in this respect makes all the difference between an article wearing badly or enduring for years. We start with hide edges, and then give a résumé of edge treatments on softer leather.

Plain hide edges

The following remarks apply to single as well as multiple thickness edges. A well-finished hide edge is one that has been bevelled back and front (with an edge beveller), stained (with dye and a dauber, or with a felt tip), waxed (with a cake of beeswax) and burnished (with an edge burnisher or something hard and smooth). Bevelling takes the rawness off a cut edge, staining does the same or can be used to make an edge more definite, waxing seals the cut fibres and helps stick them together, and burnishing compresses them and gives the edge a glossy finish.
Don't try bevelling, waxing or burnishing thin or loose-textured hide edges. They tend to splay and soften as you work on them, the exact opposite of what you want. The answer here is to lay them flat and polish hard along the edge with a rag and some saddle soap.
On bag flaps and belts a groove or line of stitching parallel to the edge adds a *je ne sais quoi*, a touch of craftsmanship. To our eyes a lot of belts and bag flaps look unfinished without one or the other.

Reinforcing and binding hide edges

On thin hide both of these treatments are strengthening; on thick hide they would simply be decorative.
The edge of a bag flap could be reinforced with a plain strip of hide (figure 58) or with a piece cut so that it makes the flap design (figure 59). In either case the reinforcing piece is appliquéd, that is glued and stitched, to the front of the flap and their edges finished together.
Binding should be done with thin, stretchy leather.

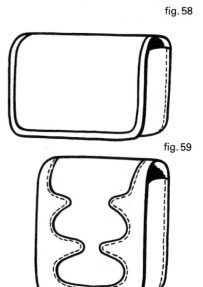

fig. 58

fig. 59

Essentially it's for protecting edges but it can be decorative as well. Where you have a double thickness edge to be bound and joined – a gusset/bag front join for example – it's better to bind each edge separately and make separate sets of stitch holes in the gusset and bag front and then stitch or lace them together, than attempt to join and bind all in the same operation using a single strip of binding (figure 60). You'll also find that applying glue to the front and back of an edge and then smoothing and stretching the binding over it works rather better than working with gluey binding. If you do decide to bind two edges with one piece of binding (figure 61) glue them together before you put the binding on, then pierce your stitch holes through all thicknesses, keeping your awl absolutely vertical as you hit it. This isn't always practical. In the long run the first method is usually easier and neater.

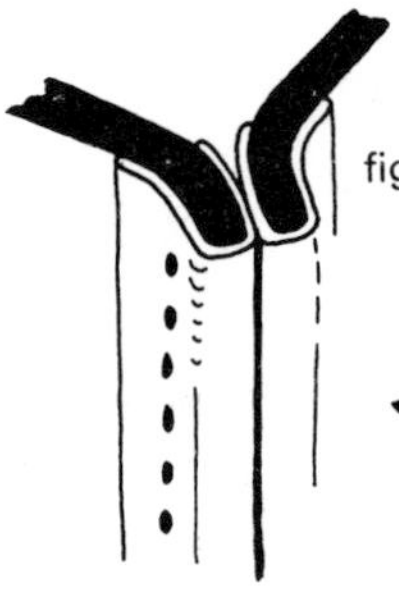

Laced hide edges

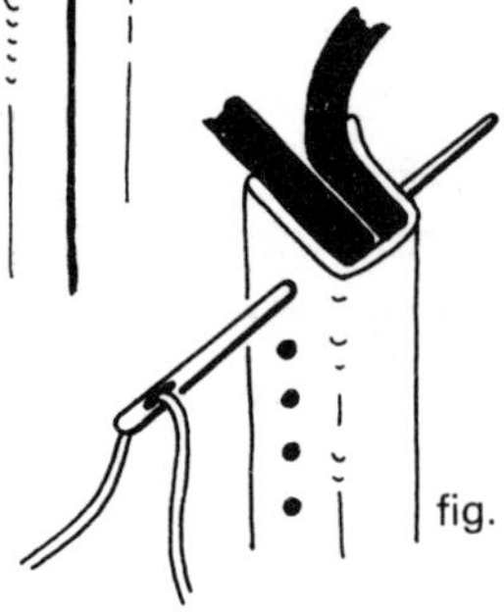

Lacing is very versatile on edges: it can define an edge in much the same way as edge dyeing or staining, it can make good strong edge joins, it can strengthen edges, it can cover up raw ones, provided they're not too thick – or do all these things at once.

Take a gusset/bag front seam on a plain hide bag. You could make the join, cover up the raw edges, protect them against scuffing and emphasize the shape of the bag all in one go with single or double loop lacing (figures 62 and 63) or Florentine lacing (figure 64). Single and double looping require fairly firm lacing but the Florentine sort is done with much wider, softer strips of leather.

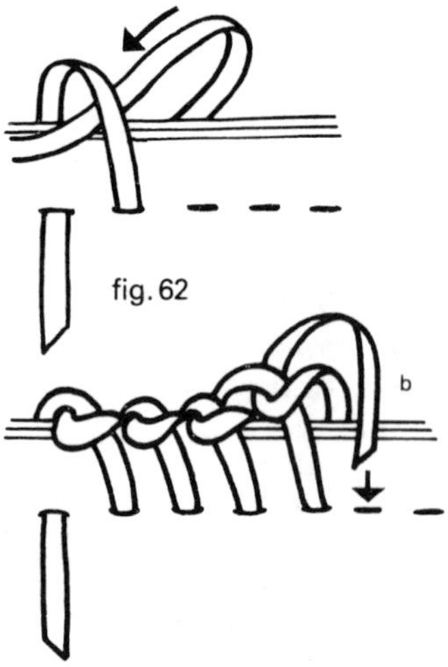

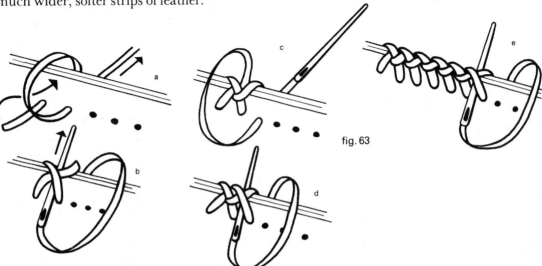

fig. 60

fig. 61

fig. 62

fig. 63

Double loop lacing is a bit tricky to start with but don't give up – it's one of the nicest edge finishes there is. You really do need a lacing needle here. Stiffened ends just won't do – you'll never get the lacing tight enough. The ratio between the length of lacing needed and the distance to be worked is about 7 to 1 for double looping, 6 to 1 for single looping and 4 to 1 for Florentine lacing. Practise until you get your lacing slanting at an angle to the edge rather than at right angles to it. For some reason it always looks more professional.

Much simpler to do, of course, is whipped lacing, the plain sort, the V sort and the X sort (figures 65, 66, 67). Then there is simple running stitch lacing (figure 68). None of these cover up as much of the edge as single or double loop or Florentine lacing, but they do make serviceable joins along edges and are decorative up to a point.

There are no weighty arguments in favour of holes or slits, just preferences. Ours is for holes, simply because they make threading easier. Slits can be cut with a single or multiple prong thonging chisel and holes with a rotary or drive punch. If you use slits make them parallel to the edge, not at an angle to it. On thick leather you may need to prise them open with an awl before you can get the lacing through. Ideally your slits/holes should be a little less than a lace width apart. Start, end and join lacing lengths in between your two thicknesses. A neat, strong way of securing the starting end is to make a slit in it and thread the other end through it (figure 69).

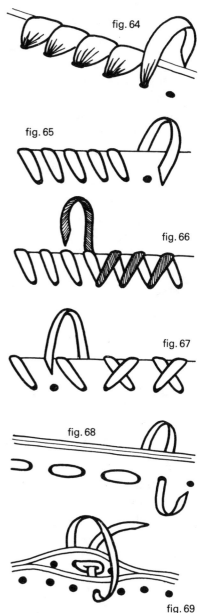

fig. 64

fig. 65

fig. 66

fig. 67

fig. 68

fig. 69

Cutwork hide edges

Cutwork edges, provided the leather is not weakened by too much slotting and slicing, are rather unusual (see, for example, the pattern used on the flap of the Shoulder Bag, page 52). They require a degree of confidence with the curved blade on the Stanley knife, which must be razor sharp. Hold the leather horizontal and the Stanley vertical, blade upwards, and draw the blade towards you through the leather following a pencilled cutting line. If that sounds too nerve-racking then think of a pattern that could be cut with various punches – rotary, wad, bag – and complemented with some sort of stamping. We suggest you use only the firmest, thickest sort of hide for cutwork. Compress and wax the edges on the flat. In most cases these will be too curved for you to be able to use an edge beveller or burnishing wheel with any success.

Other edges

There's one thing non-hide edges will do which thick hide edges won't, and that is turn under. So the simplest edge finish on other leathers is gluing, turning under and flattening with a mallet. You may need to skive the edges to make turning easier and also clip curves (figure 70). A line or two of stitching may be appropriate too. You may also need to tape your edge to prevent it stretching (see page 124).

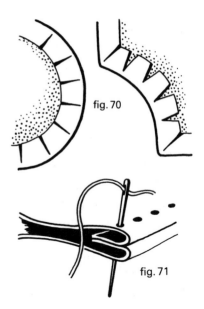

fig. 70

Double turned edges are good where thickness and firmness are needed (figure 71). With piping or fringing in them they're even more solid. But if you want less bulky double turned edges, trim the turn-under allowance off one of the edges (figures 72 and 73).

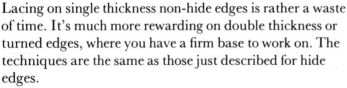

fig. 72

fig. 71

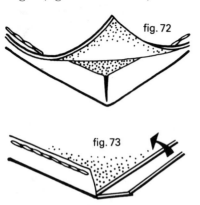

fig. 73

Lacing on single thickness non-hide edges is rather a waste of time. It's much more rewarding on double thickness or turned edges, where you have a firm base to work on. The techniques are the same as those just described for hide edges.

Non-hide edges often need reinforcing or binding. We show two ways of doing this, one purely functional, the other combining binding with cutwork (figure 74). Which brings us to cutwork edges – pinking, scalloping, fringing, and cutting or punching holes. Don't expect this sort of edge to stand up to much wear, though, unless your leather is fairly thick. Thin leather edges should be reinforced by another strip of leather on the back.

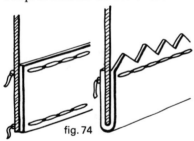

fig. 74

5 Colouring and finishes

Dyes

Before you begin Most of the leather dyes you can buy
have a spirit base, are thin like water and soak into leather
rapidly. They dry quickly to give permanent waterproof
colours. Often they're sold as powders which need to be
mixed with methylated spirit, otherwise they come ready
mixed in bottles. If you use the powder type equip yourself
with a selection of glass bottles, with tight snap-on or screw
tops, for mixing and storing. The dyes will come with
instructions on how to mix them up so scrutinize the details
carefully. You can buy a good range of colours and most of
them can be diluted to give lighter shades. Colours can also
be mixed, but we find mixing more than two colours turns
the dye muddy.

fig. 75

Dyes work best on natural vegetable tanned cowhide. They
won't take on anything with a high gloss finish. In our
experience the better the quality of the cowhide the better it
takes the dye, because it is more evenly tanned. Remember
that the original colour of the hide, anything from quite
deep pinky tones to light cream, will affect the final colour
you get. So always try out your dye on scraps of the actual
leather you plan to use. Dye all the bits and pieces that
belong to the same article with the same batch of dye *before*
you assemble them but *after* you've done all the bevelling
and cut holes and slots.

Leather dyes will penetrate just about anything, so have lots
of newspaper around and work in thin rubber gloves if you
value normal-looking hands.

Cleaning leather You're bound to have handled the
leather a fair amount before you get to the dyeing stage so it
may be a little bit greasy. Not everybody suggests that you
bother to clean leather before you dye it, but we think it's an
added insurance against uneven dyeing. It's not a great
performance – just rub the leather lightly all over with
acetone or white spirit on a non-fluff rag. Leave it to dry
before you start dyeing.

Putting on the dye Dye used straight from the bottle is
pretty concentrated. You can get away with applying it neat
on small items, but over large areas you'll end up with
streaks. So for biggish jobs, and this means bag flaps and
fronts as well as wide belt lengths, dilute the dye well and
work up to the colour you want by putting on lots of coats.
Apply each one before the previous one dries. Touch up
hole and slot edges using a paintbrush dipped in dye and if,
finally, you want to colour the edges with a darker dye use
the method shown in figure 147, page 87.

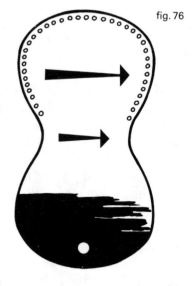

fig. 76

It's best to use a little sponge to put the dye on with but you
can use cotton wool. Get a fair amount of dye on the sponge
but not so much that it's dripping wet. Then work with
quick, even strokes from side to side across the narrowest
width of the leather. Make sure you dye the edges too. If
you've got several pieces of leather to dye it's always safest
to start on a piece that's not going to be too conspicuous in
the finished item.

Whilst the leather is still wet with dye it's difficult to tell
what's going to be a permanent blotch or streak and what
isn't. Sometimes it looks really ropy but dries out OK, so
wait and see. If it's still got streaks when it's dry then maybe
you didn't dilute the dye enough or didn't work with
sufficient dye on the sponge. To get rid of the streaks you
can dye darker, working in the opposite direction to the
streaks or rubbing round and round in little circles.

Finishing When the leather dries it'll probably look pretty
dry and dull. That's because the dye removes some of the
natural oils in the leather. Don't worry, you haven't
finished. You can rub the surface hard with a rag and
produce a fair shine. Better still, feed the leather with saddle
soap. This will enrich the colour and polish up to a beautiful
sheen.

fig. 77

Antique finish

This is a colouring that comes in a soft cream form and is
available in a range of browns and tans. You can use it on
untreated or dyed cowhide. It doesn't exactly dye so much
as tone down the existing leather colour.

You're most likely to use antique finish on carved or
stamped leather to emphasize the relief. There are two ways
of doing this. The first is to apply the cream only to the
raised parts of the leather leaving the impressed design

light. This is best done by stretching several layers of soft
rag over a small wooden block, smearing some cream
sparingly on the rag, then rubbing it over the leather.
The second way is to darken all the recesses and leave the
raised parts light. (We did this on the Screen Panels, page
49.) In this case apply the antiquing with an old toothbrush
or other stiffish brush. Put a fair amount on the brush and
apply over a small area working it well into all the crevices.
Immediately wipe off the excess – the longer it stays on the
more colour the leather will take up.
Unfortunately antiquing doesn't give a waterproof finish, so
when it's completely dry polish the leather with saddle
soap. Should you want to combine antiquing with neatsfoot
oil apply the neatsfoot a couple of hours before you antique.
If you put it on afterwards it'll just pick up the antiquing
and smear it around.

Leather paints

We've used leather paints for colouring in stamped patterns
on thick hide (see Carrying Straps, page 51) and for
painting designs on soft grain leather (see Chair, page 49).
The type we use are the ones sold for colouring shoes and
you can buy these in any number of shoe repair shops and
department stores. These paints aren't absorbed by the
leather, they merely form a surface film. Nevertheless they
are completely opaque after two or three coats even on the
darkest leather and stand up to a fair amount of flexing.
They go on evenly and smoothly and allow the grain of the
leather to show. A painted surface doesn't usually need any
extra finishing. Just buff to a good shine with a soft cloth.

Fabric dyes and paints

Use all such dyes and paints on absorbent leather surfaces,
i.e. on sueded, not grain, leather. Dylon cold dyes give good
permanent colours on light-coloured suede splits or
chamois. However, given the colour range in thin splits
there's no reason to dye whole skins except, of course, if you
wanted a tie-dye pattern. But we find it unsatisfactory to
dye a whole piece of leather by total immersion. The leather
shrinks unevenly as it dries and it's impossible to restore its
original softness and nap even by rolling and brushing. On
the other hand, dyeing and tie-dyeing small scraps of
leather for appliqué works fine.
We find printing a much more successful way of using both

Dylon cold dyes (well concentrated) and fabric paints (the sort mixable with water). The piece of printed chamois shown on page 76 was done with fabric paint and three wooden blocks. Two of the blocks were simply sections of dowel and the other shape was made up from several pieces of wooden moulding glued together. Chair and picture rail mouldings are a good source for shapes (figure 78). Print directly with the wooden surface or better still stick on some felt. This gives a more even printing surface and holds the dye or paint better. Dip the block in the colour and blot it on a damp sponge before pressing firmly onto the leather. Trial runs on scraps first, remember.

Fabric paints are supposed to be 'fixed' with a very hot iron so they don't fade in the wash. Well, hot irons and washing don't do leather much good so we miss out this stage. Nevertheless we have tried washing samples and in fact we found the colour was fast, so a spot of rain won't hurt. We can't vouch for dry cleanability.

fig. 78

Felt tips

You can use these to draw quite intricate designs on hide bags, belts and straps, etc. Strong, dark colours work best. Use spirit-based markers if you want to put on a saddle soap finish – water-based ones will smear. The chunky sort of permanent marker is also useful for colouring bevelled hide edges.

Felt tips work equally well on light-coloured suede and soft, matt grain leather. Some so-called 'permanent' markers smudge if you get them wet, so again, experiment on scraps first.

Leather used in furnishing: screen with carved leather panels;
chair with quilted design on back and seat; pouffe with reverse appliqué on seat; bolster made of suede strips laced togethe

Wallet with incised design on cover and a double tongue and loop type fastening (see page 55)

Detail of bolster end; the tie laces gathering the ends of the bolster thread through a leather-covered half ball to make a tassle

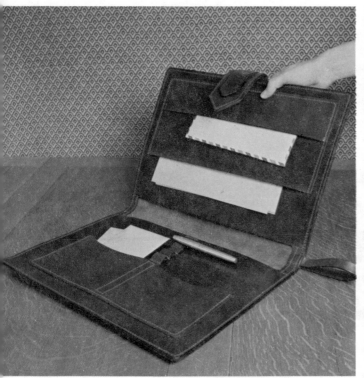

An inside view of wallet showing the pockets

Detail of quilted design on chair back

Bag combining carpet and leather,
with all-round strap handles and
laced side seams

Patchwork bag with rolled handles,
and carrying straps with
flat hide handle

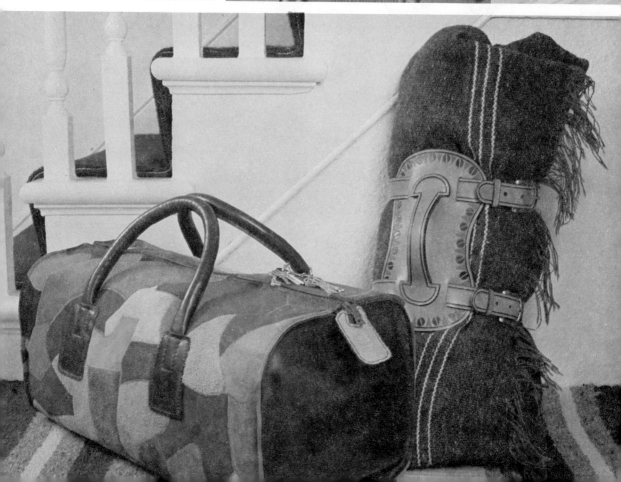

Hide shoulder bag
(the one-gusset type),
note the cutwork flap edge;
the various belts are shown
close-up in the photograph on
page 73

Leatherwork tools and
equipment, and close-up of
panel at the top of screen
(also featured on page 49)

6 Fastenings

Belts and bags are the two main articles that require special fastenings and hardware. So we've divided this chapter up accordingly to cover various fastening methods for each of them. Rivets and press studs are covered in Chapter 2.

Belt fastenings

Buckles Large heavy buckles for hide belts are usually brass and, broadly speaking, there are two main types, those with a centre bar (figure 79 – a double buckle) and those with a side bar (figure 80 – a single buckle). If you use a side bar buckle you'll need a keeper (see following section). Amongst these heftier buckles probably the largest you'll get is a 2in (5cm) one. This means it's made to take a 5cm-wide strap, though the overall width of the buckle is probably more than 2in (5cm). Other common sizes are 1½in (3·8cm) and 1¾in (4·5cm), so bear this in mind when you cut belt lengths.

Another kind of buckle that looks good with a hide belt is the flat solid variety (figure 81). These are cast with all sorts of way-out motifs and slogans on them; some are brass, some are given a bronze finish. They have a knob on the back which goes through the normal belt holes and the whole thing is fixed on as in figure 82. There are similar buckles which have a plain recessed face in which you can glue a piece of leather (carved perhaps) to match the belt. This is the type we used on the Red Laced Belt, page 73. Sometimes you come across buckles in two halves that hook together in the middle (figure 83), and there are also prongless buckles which are suitable on soft leather belts. You can make your own prongless buckles out of stiffish hide by gluing two layers together (figure 84).

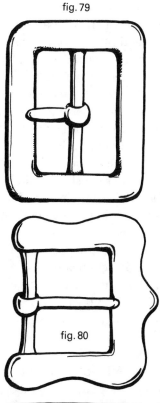

fig. 79

fig. 80

fig. 81

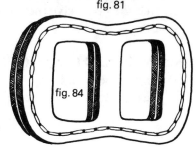

fig. 84

fig. 82

fig. 83

Small buckles are mainly of the centre or side bar type, and often come in brass or nickel. Usual sizes are ½, ¾, 1 and 1¼in (1·3, 1·9, 2·5 and 3·2cm), and sometimes ⅜ and ⅞in (1cm and 2·2cm). You may hear the term 'roller' buckle (figure 85). This is the type normally used on luggage to reduce friction on the straps.

Attaching a buckle A buckle is held on by looping the end of the belt around the centre or side bar and securing it with stitching or rivets. Estimate the length you need to make the loop and punch holes to take the rivets. Make sure the holes are lined up (figure 86). In between the two sets of holes you'll need a slot to take the buckle prong (figure 87). This slot always needs to be longer than you'd think, e.g. about 1½in (3·8cm) for the size of prong likely on a 2in (5cm) buckle. Make the slot with a bag punch if you possess one. If not, do it like this: punch holes to make either end of the slot, then join these with two parallel cuts (figure 88). Remember the slot should be equidistant between the rivet holes and plumb in the middle of the belt. Now it's plain sailing: stain the edge of the slot, fit on the buckle and set the rivets.

Some pundits suggest you skive the whole of a hide belt end before attaching a buckle. Really it's up to you. If we do any skiving at all it's just a little across the slot area to reduce bulk, and on the belt end so you don't wind up with too thick a ridge on the inside. Do this before making slots and holes.

Keepers A keeper holds the tongue end of the belt flat. It can either be a small leather loop you make yourself or a brass or nickel rectangle that you buy from a craft shop or leathercraft supplier (figure 89). You'll definitely need a keeper on a side bar buckle – they're optional with centre bar buckles. The keeper can either be loose on the belt, fixed right next to the buckle, or held between two lines of rivets (figure 90).

To make a leather keeper cut and finish a small leather strip to match the belt, skive the ends and fix them together with a small rivet.

Double ring and D-ring These make effective fastenings on narrower belts and straps. D-rings don't usually come much wider than 1¼in (3·2cm). Fix them on as in figure 91.

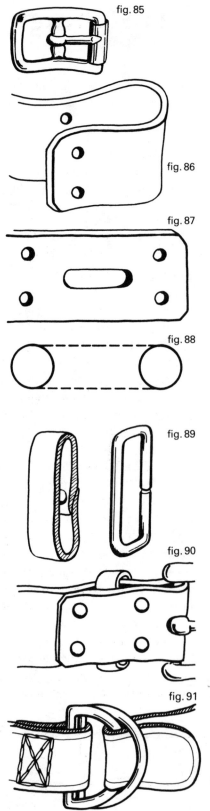

fig. 85

fig. 86

fig. 87

fig. 88

fig. 89

fig. 90

fig. 91

Hinges Go along to an ironmongers and have a good squint at some hinges to see what's suitable. Figure 92 shows a couple of designs that could be used to good effect. Occasionally you see hinges with a special removable centre pin, but mostly they're the fixed pin type. Just knock out the centre pin to separate the two halves and replace it with a screw, nail or split pin. Fix each half of the hinge to the belt using rivets through the screw holes. Hinges are sold in pairs but even so they can work out cheaper than a heavy brass buckle. We used a hinge fastening on the Green Belt, page 73.

Locks Folio-case locks make unconventional belt fastenings, and are stocked by some leathercraft suppliers (figure 93). Rivet through the screw holes or use the prong fastenings on the lock.

Tie ends There's nothing revolutionary about this method. Depending on what leather the belt is made of either cut the ends into tie strips, use the ends of thonging already woven through the belt (figure 94), or actually add on some tie lengths. The ties can be plaited, knotted or beaded.

Bag fastenings

Tongue and loop (figure 95) This is a flat closure, so it's good on wallets too. The loop part is made like a belt keeper only it goes through slots cut in the bag front (figure 97).

Double tongue and loop (figure 96) This is more thief-proof than a single tongue and loop. The loop is fixed in the bag front as in figure 97. Then you cut a large tongue with a slot in it to go over the loop, and a small tongue to go on top of the large one and through the loop. (This is the type used for the Wallet, page 50.) Sew the tongues together, then sew the large one to the bag or wallet flap.

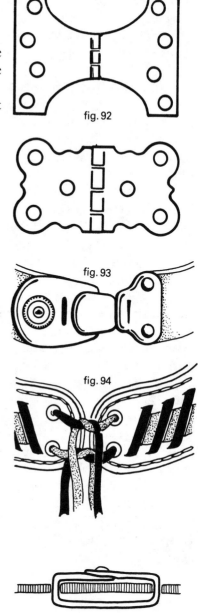

fig. 92

fig. 93

fig. 94

fig. 97

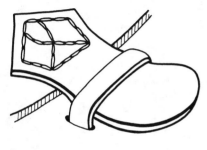

fig. 95

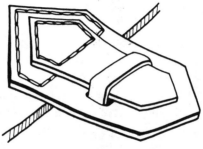

fig. 96

Loop and toggle (figure 98) This is like a do-it-yourself turnlock. Fix the toggle vertically to the bag front with some leather thonging. Cut a horizontal slot in the bag flap big enough to take the toggle.

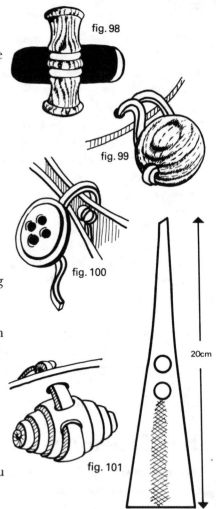

fig. 98

fig. 99

Loop and bead/toggle/button This type just involves a leather loop that goes over a bead, toggle or button (figure 99). It can be used to secure a flap or to keep an open top closed. An alternative is to dispense with the loop and just use a length of thonging that twists round a button (figure 100).

To make the kind of leather toggle shown in figure 101, here's how. Cut a sort of long V as in the illustration and make the two holes. Spread some glue over the crosshatched area on both sides. Roll up the leather starting at the wide end. When you get to the holes poke a knitting needle or something through to stretch them, poke the end of the toggle through and pull tight. Use the rest of the thin end to attach the toggle to the bag.

fig. 100

20cm

Strap and buckle Depending on the shape of the flap, the buckle can either be fixed to the bag front on a small strap, or to the bottom of the gusset as on our Shoulder Bag, page 52.

Turnlock (figure 102) This is a piece of hardware that you can buy from most leathercraft suppliers. You simply cut slits in the leather for the prongs, then bend and hammer them flat on the reverse side.

fig. 101

fig. 102

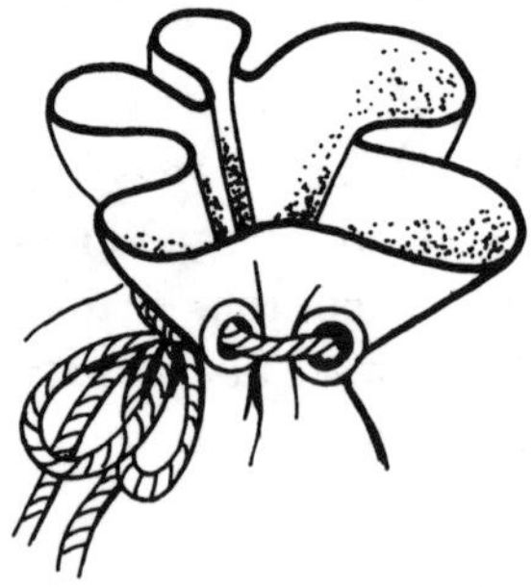

fig. 103

Draw strings (figure 103) This type of closure is really only viable on soft, floppy bags. Use large eyelets if you can get them.

Zips Zips are suitable for bags without flaps, see Patchwork Bag, page 51.

Flap and strap (figure 104) This is really a variation on the tongue and loop method, only the tongue is an integral part of the flap and goes through a strap added to the bag front. Figures 104a and b show you what we mean.

fig. 104

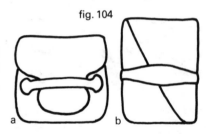

a   b

7 Handles

We've discussed straps for shoulder bags on pages 98–9, so here we'll run through the easier types of handle to make for heavier bags, e.g. holdalls and shopping bags.

Flat handles

1 We used one type of flat handle on the Carrying Straps, page 51. This is the sort suitable for horizontal flat surfaces like the top of a flap on a bag or briefcase. Use heavy cowhide (3–4mm) and cut one complete handle piece (figure 105a) and another piece the same width but shorter (figure 105b). A good average length for a is 21cm (8½in). If you only have thin cowhide, glue several layers together. Skive the ends of b well over the crosshatched area. Glue a and b together – with the grain side of b against the flesh side of a – and roughen up both surfaces before you spread glue on them. Round off the edges of the handle part with an edge beveller so that it's comfortable to hold, then wax and burnish the edges well. It's not structurally necessary but it looks good if you stitch along the edges of the part you hold as well as round the ends. Stitch the handle on using pre-punched holes and strong thread. As you do so, arch the leather up in the middle so the handle is easy to grip (figure 106).

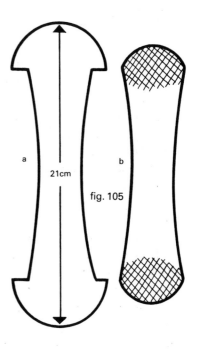

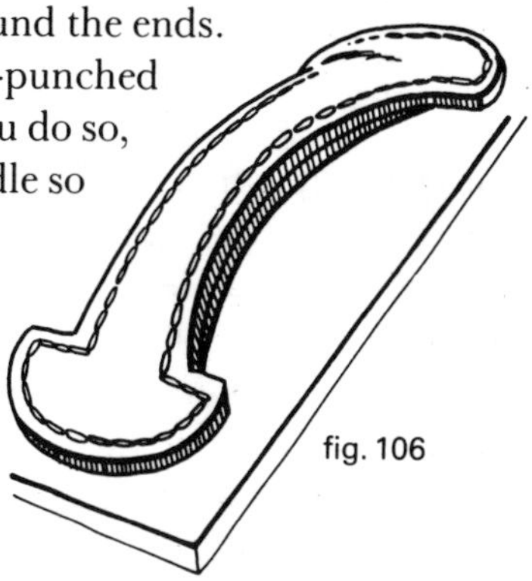

a   b
21cm
fig. 105

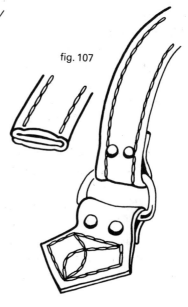

fig. 106

fig. 107

2 If your bag is in softer leather, and you need a handle to match, cut a wide strip of the leather, fold it in three lengthways and stitch along the edges. Then rivet the ends round D-rings. To attach the handle, cut some leather tabs (shaped to complement the bag), fix these to the D-rings with rivets, then stitch the tabs securely to the bag (figure 107).

3 This is a hide version of the flat pairs of plastic or wooden handles you can buy for beach bags. For each handle cut two identical pieces of hide (figure 108a) – adapt the shape to suit your bag. Glue the pieces together, flesh sides facing, stitch around the edges, then glue the handle over the top of the bag and stitch (figure 108b).

Rolled handles

These make really comfortable handles, look very professional and are pretty simple to make. We used a rolled handle on the Patchwork Bag, page 51. Obviously it's easier to sew this type of handle onto a flat backing, so if you can bring yourself to decide exactly where they should go before you assemble the bag so much the better. If not, you'll just have to fight with needle and thread in the recesses of the made-up bag – not impossible but difficult. You need a reasonably strong but flexible grain leather. To reinforce the body of the handle you'll require thick cord or rope. If you can't lay your hands on the right thickness then make it up from several pieces of cord bound firmly together with strips of leather or fabric. Make sure the finished thickness isn't too lumpy or it will show through the leather. Cut the cord long enough to reinforce the main body of the handle, and flatten the ends well by pounding with the mallet.

Cut a piece of leather wide enough to go round the cord plus a generous seam allowance. Glue the leather round the cord, make the stitch holes with an awl and mallet and get going with thread and harness needles. Trim close to the stitching (figure 109).

There are three ways of treating the ends of the handle. The simplest is to cut the ends to shape, splay them out and stitch them directly to the bag (figure 110). Use a piece of leather on the back of the bag as reinforcement, so that you're actually stitching through three layers. Alternatively, trim and splay the leather ends out as before and roughly stitch them to the bag. Then glue and stitch another piece of leather over the ends of the handle (figure 111) and reinforce the back as before. This is the way we attached the handles on the Patchwork Bag, page 105.

The third way is to loop and rivet (or stitch) the handle ends round D-rings or rectangles, and use separate leather tabs to attach the D-rings to the bag (figure 112). On the whole, stitched tabs are stronger than riveted ones because they spread the stress over a larger area.

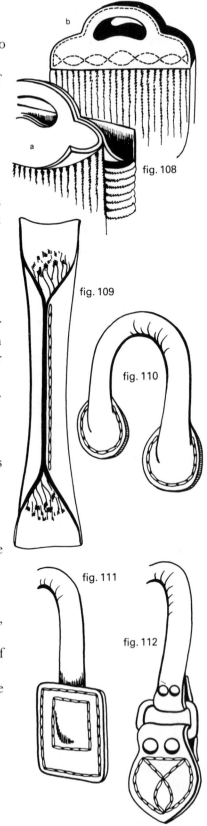

fig. 108

fig. 109

fig. 110

fig. 111

fig. 112

Plaited handles

Three and five-strand, closed-end plaits are described on pages 81–2. Either type make strong decorative handles. We used three-strand plaits for the handles on the Carpet Bag, page 51. They can be used as flat handles (figure 113), or, because the plait can be coaxed round a curve, as upright handles (figure 114). Because the plaits do 'give' a bit it's best not to put them on bags that are going to carry enormous weights!

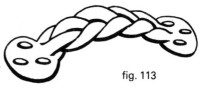

fig. 113

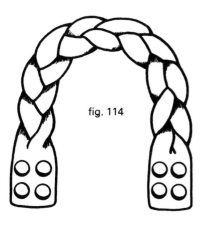

fig. 114

Strap handles

Handles that go right round a bag are exceptionally strong because there is no single point that takes all the weight (figure 115). Either stitch them to the bag all the way round, or rivet them at intervals. The handles on the Carpet Bag, page 51, are this sort, except that they disappear inside the bag temporarily so as not to cover up too much of the carpet pattern.

Have a look at 'Attaching straps' on page 98 for other handle ideas.

fig. 115

Bought handles

These range from the flat sort in wood or plastic already mentioned under 'Flat handles' to ready-made attaché or suitcase handles obtainable from some leathercraft suppliers. Some haberdashery departments stock large metal rings or shaped metal bars which you can include in a hemmed bag top (figure 116).

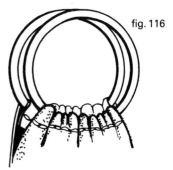

fig. 116

8 Carving and stamping

Impressing a design into the grain side of dampened leather
so that parts of the pattern are left in relief is variously and
confusingly called leather carving, modelling or tooling. In
brief, leather carving means outlining the design with a cut
in the leather, then pressing down one side of the cut plus
whole areas within the design, thus leaving parts in bold
relief. There are special tools produced for doing this – a
cutting knife called a swivel knife and various flattening
tools that you hit with a mallet. These are the tools we'll be
talking about here, and most of this kind of work is done on
thick hide. The picture on page 49 shows a carved panel
and the tools used to do it.
Now there are other sorts of tools around called modelling
or tooling tools. You don't hit these with a mallet. You just
use them with hand pressure to model the leather surface,
and you don't have to use them in conjunction with a cut.
So, you could use one or two of these to produce a simple
impressed line design. We mention them only because you
may find a couple of them useful for emphasizing areas of
your carved design. The moral is, don't ignore them just
because they're not leather carving tools *per se*.

Leather A natural vegetable tanned cowhide is the best
leather to use for carving – in fact it is sometimes called
'tooling hide'. To avoid any confusion when you buy make
it clear what you want the leather for. The best thickness to
start on is somewhere between 2·5–3·5mm – don't try on
anything thinner till you're really expert.

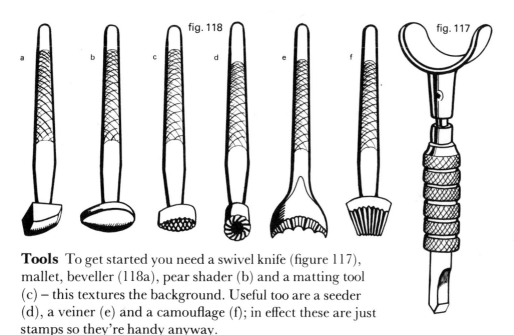

fig. 118

fig. 117

Tools To get started you need a swivel knife (figure 117), mallet, beveller (118a), pear shader (b) and a matting tool (c) – this textures the background. Useful too are a seeder (d), a veiner (e) and a camouflage (f); in effect these are just stamps so they're handy anyway.

All these tools, except the swivel knife, come in different sizes, so more on this and how to use them in a minute. (Incidentally, we've told you how we used them – if you find you get good results handling them slightly differently, fine.) Quite often leathercraft suppliers offer carving tools as a kit, which is quite a good way to buy and saves you the problem of wondering what sizes to get.

Preparing the leather Leather will only cut easily and take up and hold an imprint if it is damp. So, before work with any of the tools and even before tracing on your design, you need to dampen the leather – to 'case' it is the proper term. Do this with water and a small piece of sponge. Dampen the flesh side first then the grain side, working as evenly as you can. The sponge should be pretty damp but not wringing wet. Don't start cutting right away, leave the leather a minute or so to allow the water to penetrate. A few trials and errors will soon tell you when the leather is ready to work. You'll need to redampen the leather occasionally. One thing, when you flip the leather over to dampen the flesh side, make sure your working surface is clean and free from bits – the grain side of leather picks up marks very easily. Talking of which, watch out for fingernail marks whilst you're working with the tools.

What about a design? It's not too difficult to work out your own design, as we did for the panels of the Screen, on page 49. Alternatively you can buy plastic stencils that you simply press onto the leather to transfer a design, or there are books of patterns you can copy. Opposite is a simple flower design which we've drawn through all the main working stages just so you can see what we're talking about.

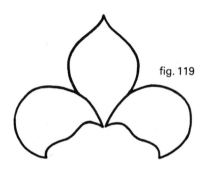

fig. 119

Transferring a pattern If you've made up your own design or chosen one from a book of patterns you'll need to transfer it to the leather. Tracing paper isn't ideal because, of course, you're working on a damp surface (remember the leather should be cased) but it is possible to use it for small designs. A better alternative is to use some waxed paper – the semi-transparent type used for wrapping food. Ideally use something called tracing film. This is a sort of polyester film that has a matt side that'll take pencil or ink and a glossy side that won't. This should be available from an art shop which stocks graphics supplies. Anyway, whatever you use, trace your design onto it.

Lay the tracing glossy or waxed side down on the cased leather and hold it in place with mapping or drawing pins at the corners. Go over the lines with a biro or pencil. When you lift the tracing you'll find the lines are perfectly reproduced on the leather because it's been bruised and therefore darkened where you pressed with the pencil. Right, now you can get going with the swivel knife.

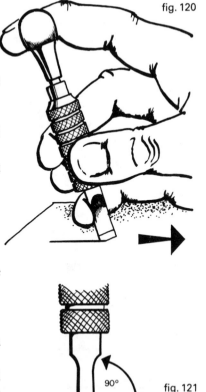

fig. 120

Cutting with the swivel knife It's called a swivel knife because the barrel that holds the blade can rotate, making it easy to cut curves. The knife is held as in figure 120 so that the index finger can exert downward pressure on the yoke; the thumb, second and third finger hold and turn the barrel as necessary; the little finger is held against the blade to help control it, and the side of the hand should be in contact with the leather.

The cut is made just with the corner of the blade, so the knife is held at a slant and pulled towards you (figure 120). All cuts are made by pulling the knife towards you and pressing down on the yoke at the same time. The depth of cut should be about half the thickness of the leather. Maybe this sounds complicated but all becomes clear when you've got a swivel knife in your hand.

It's important to keep the blade upright when you cut (figure 121) otherwise you can undercut, which doesn't look too good and makes later stages difficult. It's tricky to go over cuts again accurately, so try not to. Have a really good work-out on scrap leather first. Swivel the barrel of the knife to get round curves and turn the leather so you can

90°   fig. 121

complete the curve in one action. If cutting gets difficult, maybe the knife needs sharpening or the leather needs redamping. There are different types of blade for the swivel knife, wider ones for really bold designs, and small, angled jobs for more intricate work.

After cutting, the flower design should look like figure 122.

Bevelling The next stage is to push down one side of the cut. You do this with the beveller and mallet. We find a medium size beveller most useful. Insert the toe of the beveller in the cut. Now work it towards you a fraction at a time and strike the mallet between moves (figure 123). Practise till you can do this smoothly. This will produce a darkened bevelled slope with the deepest part next to the cut. Keep the beveller upright or sloped just slightly away from you as you work.

The flower design now looks something like figure 124.

Shading Shading or contouring is done with the pear shader. We find a medium and a really small pear shader most useful. This tool has two functions – to produce shading within raised parts of the design, e.g. on petals and leaves, etc. and to flatten background areas prior to finishing them with the matting tool (figure 125). Use the shader with the point towards you and work it towards you striking with the mallet as for the beveller. Again practice will reveal all. Occasionally, instead of hitting the shader we use hand pressure just to sharpen up the edges of shaded areas and also to help flatten the background areas. This is where a moulding tool could be handy.

Matting Having got the background areas flattened as best you can with the shader, you now texture them with the matting tool. The object is to give the background an even tone and create a texture that automatically darkens the background leaving everything else in relief. As with the other tools, work towards you with the point towards you, but twist the tool slightly between taps so you don't get a regular tool pattern appearing.

A small matting tool is the most useful because you can winkle it into tiny corners, and actually it lessens the chance of getting a tool pattern. Once you get going it doesn't take long to do quite large areas of background.

Voilà, a nearly finished flower (figure 126).

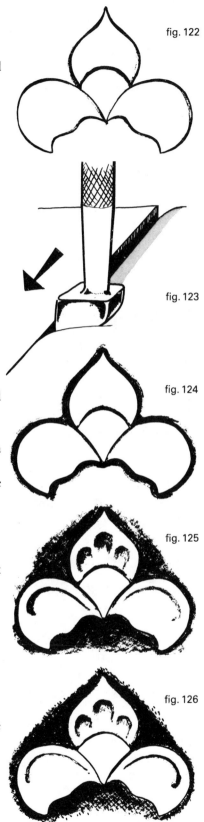

fig. 122

fig. 123

fig. 124

fig. 125

fig. 126

That's about it. You can use the swivel knife to add decorative cuts and flourishes if you like. Use the seeder for flower centres and the veiner or camouflage for leaf and petal markings (see final flower in figure 127). Besides the main tools we used a couple of seeders and a camouflage for our Screen panels, page 49. The circles round the edges were made with a piece of metal pipe.

fig. 127

Antiquing This is covered on page 46. Obviously the antique finish will darken the cuts and background most but it will also colour the raised parts. If you want these to take up less colour, bunch up a rag into a firm flat wodge, put on a little saddle soap, and rub really well over the carving. This will give the raised parts a bit of resistance to the antiquing.

Carving with other tools

Apart from the techniques and tools just discussed, you can produce beautiful incised line patterns using a groover, race or gouge. The grooves can be coloured with dye (applied with a paintbrush) or a spirit-based felt tip pen, or left light against a dark background. In all cases burnish along the grooves with something hard and smooth, e.g. a spoon handle. Other effects can be obtained by dyeing areas enclosed by the grooves different colours. The Coiled Bangle on page 73 illustrates this technique.
The design on the cover of the Wallet, page 50, was in fact done with an edge groover.

Stamping

Like carving, stamping is done on cased leather. Bought stamps and home-made ones are given a mention on page 30. You can stamp before or after dyeing. If you stamp before dyeing the dye probably won't take as well in the impressions as on the surrounding leather. With care you can avoid getting dye in the stamped areas altogether, which creates some very interesting effects.

9 Adding to leather

Appliqué

Appliqué simply means fixing one piece of material on top of another piece, or backing a cut-out area (reverse appliqué) to achieve a decorative effect. The advantage of leather over fabric appliqué is, of course, that there's no problem with fraying edges.

The best leather for appliqué is soft thin grain leather or suede split, so hang on to any bits and pieces left over from things you've made. If you need to repeat a motif accurately then cut out a pattern in thin card, a template, and draw round it on the wrong side of the leather, otherwise just sketch the shape you want straight onto the leather. Use a really sharp pair of scissors to cut out your shapes. Lightly glue the pieces in position then stitch them on round the edges (figure 128). If the thickness of the leather isn't prohibitive you can use a sewing machine to do this, otherwise handstitch the edges using small running, overcast, herringbone or blanket stitches (see page 37). The Pouffe on page 49 has a reverse appliqué design on the seat, and one of the pockets on page 75 has an appliquéd daisy motif.

Appliqué isn't only suitable on soft leather surfaces. It could be used on hide, to decorate a belt for example. In this case use pre-punched stitch holes and make a feature of the stitching.

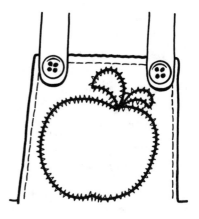

fig. 128

Beadwork

If you've ever seen examples of African or American Indian beadwork you may be inspired to try your hand at it too. Smothering vast areas with close beadwork is a bit daunting, but small areas on belts, chokers, wristbands (see the one on page 73) and garment edges can be simple to do and eye-catching too. The little African beads are the nicest to work with and come in a range of beautiful colours. Most craft shops have them.

There are two ways of sewing beads to leather. One way is

to string dozens on a length of button- or thin nylon-thread (normal sewing thread is a bit feeble), thread up a needle with similar thread and 'couch' the string of beads onto the leather. This means you bring the needle through to the right side and make a small stitch over the stringing thread between every third or fourth bead (figure 129). This method is good for doing line designs in beads.

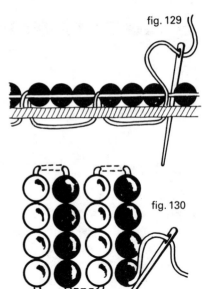

fig. 129

fig. 130

To make up solid blocks of beads you use the same thread to string the beads and attach them. Bring the needle through to the right side, thread on a few beads (yes, this means you have to keep on unthreading the needle!) then stitch back through the leather and so on (figure 130). This is how we did the blue and white part of the Beadwork Wristband, page 73. The red border was 'couched' on.

We've found no really quick way of stringing up these little beads. A fine needle makes it quicker, but if it's small enough to go through the beads it won't usually take button or nylon thread. So, you end up having to poke them on the thread one by one – actually this doesn't take too long and it's very therapeutic!

Beads also look good on leather fringing or on the ends of thong ties. Either knot the end of the thong or fringe to hold the bead on, or neater still, thread on the bead, cut the leather to a point, smear with glue and poke the end back into the bead hole.

Embroidery

We're not going to tell you how to do dozens of embroidery stitches. Nevertheless, embroidery is a perfectly valid way of decorating leather. Remember all those embroidered sheepskin coats and waistcoats from Afghanistan?

On thin leather use any of the usual embroidery threads plus either a leather needle (take care not to cut previous stitches) or a normal sharp needle. On hide, make stitch holes with an awl and use a tough non-fray thread and a harness needle. Pre-punched stitch holes limit the kind of embroidery possible so probably bold outline stitching is best. Anyway, have a look at the Embroidered Braces on page 74.

Metalwork

Studs, eyelets, rivets and pieces of metal strip can all be used to make designs on belts, straps, waistcoats and garment edges. Have a look at the Metalwork Wristband on page 73 and the Green Belt on the same page.

10 Other techniques

No order of merit is implied by the order in which these 'other techniques' appear. They're all legitimate and attractive ways of using leather. There are a few more obscure ways, but we leave those to your curiosity.

Patchwork

This can be done with leftovers or with leather bought specially for the purpose. For the Patchwork Bag on page 51 we bought several pounds of shoe upper scraps and used them suede side out – the suede side is often a lot more attractive than the leather side. Nice scraps can be difficult to get hold of, because they get snapped up by makers of fancy handbags. Some merchants, though, sell returns from their larger customers and may let you rummage out the colours you want. All your scraps should be of similar thickness. The suede side is usually lighter and brighter than the grain side, so you have two colours for the price of one.

For ideas on patchwork patterns we suggest you consult a book on the subject. Where leather patchwork differs from the fabric type is in the way it's sewn together. There's no need to turn edges under, for instance. Simply butt them together and lace or sew across the join, or overlap them and stitch or lace through both thicknesses. We recommend you work on a backing of some sort – skiver or upholstery cowhide, muslin or thick denim depending on the finished thickness you want – if you use the abutted edge method. Glue your pieces to the backing, or to each other if you're using the overlap method, before you make stitch holes or start stitching. Any of the fancy stitches on page 37, interpreted in thread or lacing, can be used for joining the patches.

As it happened the combined thickness of the leather and the denim backing used for the Patchwork Bag was just within the capacity of our sewing machine, so we did close zigzag stitch over all the abutted edges. It got a bit tricky stitching in the middle of such a large area, though. That's why we suggest making the body of the bag in two pieces (see page 105).

Cutwork

You'll find a paragraph or two on this subject in Chapter 4. A Stanley knife (with curved blade for cutting curves and a straight one for cutting straight lines) and various hole- or slot-cutting punches are the implements you'll need. If you want to make a cut in the middle of a piece of hide you'll have to work the blade through the leather first. Do this by repeatedly scoring along one of the cutting lines.

On thin leather it's advisable to back cut-out areas with skiver or something equally thin. Even on hide, backing can serve a useful purpose. The Brown Cutwork Belt on page 73 has a black backing which, as well as serving as a lining, gives the pattern the appearance of being deeply carved rather than cut out. The Sandals on page 76 also have a cutwork panel appliquéd to the uppers – structurally it's not necessary but it creates interest. A cutwork upper without a backing would not be strong enough, unless of course the cut areas were kept extremely small.

Carefully dyeing cut edges, with a felt tip or dye and a small dauber, creates a strong relief effect if the body of the article is left light or natural.

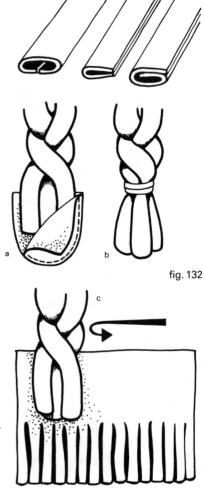

fig. 131

fig. 132

a

b

c

Plaiting

This is a technique which has many uses. Instructions on making 3- and 5-strand closed-end plaits are given on pages 81–2. This type of plait is suitable for belts, wristbands, handles, shoulder straps or wherever there is advantage in having flat, single thickness ends rather than the three separate strands you get with ordinary plaiting.

Ordinary plaits can be made from flat, single thickness strips, the same folded and glued as in figure 131, or the same folded to make three thicknesses. It all depends whether you want a flat plait or a podgy one. The narrow plait lengths round the strap slots and over some of the seams on the Carpet Bag (page 51) are of the flat, single thickness variety. For tying the waist of the Pouffe (page 49), though, we made a stronger, fatter type of plait with double thickness strands.

Plait ends can be neatened by sewing them into an end tab (figure 132a), or binding them with a narrow strip of leather (figure 132b) or small length of fringe (figure 132c).

Quilting

There are two sorts of quilting: ordinary and Italian. There's an example of the ordinary sort on the Chair (page 49) and of the Italian sort on the spectacle case, photographed with the skirt pockets on page 75.

fig. 133

Whereas ordinary quilting (figure 133) consists of sewing a design through three thicknesses (a thin top layer, a layer of padding and a backing layer), Italian quilting involves poking little pieces of padding in between two layers, into spaces enclosed by stitching (figure 134). Thus in ordinary quilting the whole padded area looks plump, with the stitching sitting in its own valleys, and in Italian quilting only the areas enclosed by the stitching look plump. For the best results use a thin, soft, stretchy leather.

fig. 134

Ordinary quilting In some ways ordinary quilting is fiddlier than Italian quilting because one has to ensure that the layers don't move relative to one another as you stitch. First, transfer your design to the right side of your leather with a sharp pencil (this makes reasonably visible marks on both suede and grain leather). Tracing through tracing paper with a blunt instrument doesn't leave a clear enough mark, so use a template to draw round, or draw your design freehand or with the aid of a ruler, compass, etc. Now place your leather on top of your padding (we use the terylene sort) and backing (we use a cotton fabric or muslin). Tack along the lines you have drawn – yes, tack with big running stitches and a fine ordinary needle and thread – through all three thicknesses. It's a good insurance to tack all round the edges of the panel too. Now do your quilting stitching proper – small running stitches with a leather needle and button thread or Sylko 40, if you're hand stitching. Machine stitching makes a good job of quilting provided your design is fairly simple.

Italian quilting Glue your quilting leather and backing (a firm weave cotton fabric will do) together round the edges. Draw your design (it must be one with smallish areas completely enclosed by stitching) on the backing side and stitch along the drawn lines with running stitch (by hand or machine). Now make small slits here and there in the backing, inside the stitched areas, and poke wisps of cotton wool into the spaces between the backing and the leather (a knitting needle or cocktail stick does the trick). When you have finished poking in the stuffing, oversew the openings to stop it coming out.

The spectacle case on page 75 has a very simple Italian quilted design on the back and front, and piping in the side seams. Turn the edges of the quilted back and front pieces under all round, glue the piping in place (around the top edges as well) and saddle stitch the sides and bottom together through all thicknesses. Make a fabric lining by sewing two pieces of fabric together round the edges. Slip it inside the leather, turn the top edges under so they cannot fray and slip stitch them to the leather.

Weaving

Our use of weaving in this book is limited to a single pocket photographed on page 75. Not that we mean any disparagement to the technique. You'll see from page 135 that it has applications for seating; straps of thick hide (with beautifully finished edges and ends, of course!) can be nailed to a stout wooden stool, chair or bed frame. Making screen panels of woven hide strips works very well too. Panels of weaving done in thinner leather look good on bag flaps, dungarees and pinafore fronts, cushions, etc. Alternate strips of grain and suede, as on the pocket in the photograph, make beautiful textures.

Whatever leather you use, start your weaving by butting all the 'across' strips against one another and securing them at both ends, with sellotape or nails depending on the context. Weave the first 'down' strip through the middle (figure 135) and work out towards the sides, securing the ends by some temporary means (sellotape again or tacks) as you work – you may need to splay them out a bit or push them up tighter before you secure them finally.

One can produce some very intriguing patterns working with two colours. Alternating them in both the 'across' and 'down' directions creates a chessboard effect. The houndstooth check effect on the pocket is the result of alternating two strips of black and two strips of beige in both directions. Still more exciting patterns emerge if you alternate two black and two beige across and one black and one beige down. Working out all the permutations is a clear case for juggling with strips of coloured paper rather than laboriously filling in squares on graph paper.

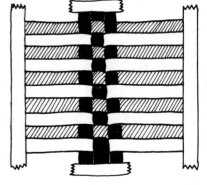

fig. 135

Moulding

This is a very easy and successful technique for using up those expensive scraps of sole leather. If you soak sole leather in lukewarm water for up to fifteen minutes it becomes soft enough to mould into various shapes. If allowed to dry naturally and kept in shape while it dries, it retains a shape very well. Always use the grain side outside – that's the way the leather 'grew' in the first place so it takes more kindly to moulding that way. The coiled bangle on page 73 was dyed and incised before soaking. The other one was branded with a soldering iron in the dry moulded state. Use something non-marking (a wide strip of cardboard or polythene secured with sellotape) to hold the leather round a mould of some kind – (a jam jar, milk bottle, aerosol can). Careful how you handle the leather when it's wet – it bruises easily and the marks remain visible even when the leather is dry.

11 Making patterns

This is a tricky chapter – that's why it's nice and short!
Making patterns, except in a very specific context, is not an
entirely logical process. There are no recipes which say do
this, this and this, and bingo! there's your pattern. So, we'll
just say what *we* find most useful.

If we're making clothes we usually buy ready-made
patterns of the appropriate size, and adapt them as the
mood takes us. We've also bought glove and hat patterns
from two of the suppliers listed in the Appendix. For other
items which have to 'fit', sandals and moccasins, for
example, we've given hints on how to make your own
patterns. Fit is irrelevant when it comes to bags, wallets,
cushions and so forth, so we've summarized construction
alternatives rather than given exact patterns.

The remarks which follow, therefore, apply mainly to bags
and other non-fitted items.

1 Start the ideas flowing by noticing what your friends are
carrying their belongings around in, what's in the shops and
magazines, what's on show in a local history museum, etc.
If you can, handle articles to see how they are put together.
Don't be humbugged by the scale of a thing. A large bag
could be scaled down to purse size, or a note-case enlarged
to folio size, and so on.

2 It's no good trying to design anything until you have a
clear vision of what you want. A truism, we know, but that's
how it is. The most successful designs are usually those one
'sees' clearest right from the beginning. Drawing and
redrawing are sometimes the only way to extract an idea
from your head. Sometimes, though, an idea crystallizes
better if you drape and fold and generally fiddle around
with the leather itself.

3 Once your idea is clear, work it out full size on paper or
card or muslin or felt, whatever gives the best imitation of
the leather you plan to use. Felt is best where a good 'fit' is
necessary, for sandals, moccasins, etc. Remember to add a
seam allowance for plain and overlap seams (see page 35).
We never find making mini models of things very useful.

Bangles (*left to right*): *top* beaded; spiral covered; metalwork; 5-plait;
bottom moulded coil; laced covered; moulded with burnt design

left to right Green belt with metal decoration and hinge fastening;
red laced belt; belt ends; brown cutwork belt;
plain length used for carrying straps (photograph page 51); yellow belt with burnt design

above Tunic with coloured laces threaded through neck and wrist openings; see neck opening detail

left Detail of embroidered braces

top right Waistcoat with bound-type buttonholes and pocket slits, and top-stitched seams; the back view shows buckle straps and gingham lining

right A panel of pockets, one woven, one gusseted with a top flap, one with zip closure; note the little triangles reinforcing the top of each pleat; the raised design on the spectacle case is Italian quilting

On the moccasins
note the heel tabs and
the way the tie laces
thread through the flaps;
we used a layer of
hide and a layer of
micro soling to make the
soles

Sandals with cutwork
appliquéd to uppers and
low wedge heels,
the last on which
we pounded the soles and
topsoles together; and a
fringed chamois cloth
which was printed with
the blocks shown on the
left

4 Don't get too obsessed by colour. Nine times out of ten you'll not be able to buy the exact colour you want, and unless you are working with natural hide, there's little you can do about it. A really good design has little to do with colour and everything to do with basic shape and construction.

5 We find coloured paper much quicker than crayons or paints for working out complicated colour schemes. For the lacing on the Tunic, page 74, we shuffled lots of little red, green and brown pieces of paper around on a full-size drawing of the neck facing until we found a pleasing pattern. We went through the same process for the quilted panel on the Chair (page 49) and for some of the bangles and belts.

6 Most shapes, if you analyse them, are a combination of straight lines and arcs of a circle. Make squares really square, rectangles perfectly rectangular. Don't guess at right-angled corners; use a set square, or something you know is perfectly square, to draw them. Use a plate, saucer or coin to draw rounded corners. Use a piece of string to measure the length of curves (this is something you may have to do if you're working out a bag pattern, see page 100).

7 For symmetrical patterns, fold a piece of flimsy paper or tracing paper in half, draw your design on one half, fold the paper over and trace the other half of the design (figure 138). The same process is just as useful for drawing very simple symmetrical shapes, bag flaps for example.

8 To transfer your pattern to the leather you can either make a template of it in thick card, and draw round it on the leather with a pencil or biro, or, if the shapes concerned are very simple, draw them straight on the leather, making the appropriate measurements as you draw. The latter is a bit risky on hide because one usually draws the pattern on the grain side. This makes flaws and discolorations easier to avoid and results in a cleaner cut than one made along a line drawn on the flesh side. On grain leather and splits, though, it's standard practice to mark cutting lines, in biro, on the wrong side, i.e. not the side visible in the finished article.

And that's about all we can tell you. There is little point giving patterns for articles which have to be adapted to fit all sizes of wearer – sandals and clothes, for example. Where appropriate we have given measurements which indicate the general size of an article, e.g. Pouffe, Bolster, Carrying Straps, Carpet Bag, Shoulder Bag, and so on.

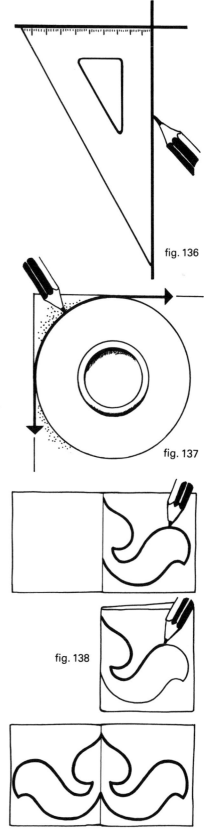

fig. 136

fig. 137

fig. 138

part two
Things to make

Wristbands

Small items like wristbands, bangles and watch straps are ideal for trying out your skills economically. They're good practice for cutting leather, finishing edges, setting fastenings and buckles and experimenting with decorating techniques. The following wristbands (photographed on page 73) illustrate various ways of using and decorating leather.

5-strand closed-end plait

Cut a strap the size shown in figure 139a from 3mm-thick vegetable tanned cowhide. Then cut the slits. Before you go any further do a trial plait following stages b and c in figure 139. You'll see that the ends look wider than the plaited bit, so cut them down to reduce them to roughly the width of the plait.

Now unplait the strap and bevel all edges – yes, along the slits too, back and front. Then dye the leather and darken the edges with a paintbrush and dye (use a pipe cleaner to get into the corners) or a felt tip pen (spirit-based). Polish the strap with saddle soap and finish the edges (see page 41 on how to finish plain hide edges). Finally, plait the strap and add a press stud fastening.

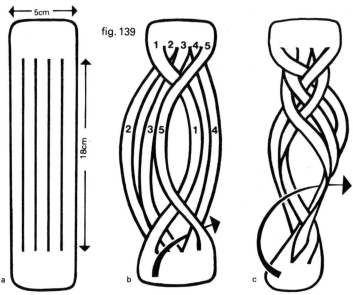

fig. 139

3-strand closed-end plait Again working with 3mm-thick cowhide, cut a strap with slits as shown in figure 140a. Repeat all the stages given above and plait as shown in stages b to e in figure 140.

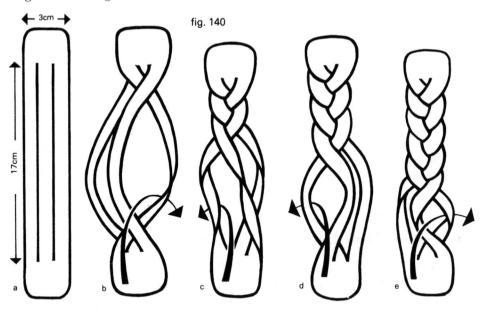

fig. 140

Longer and wider closed-end plaits The stages in figures 139 and 140 give, as it were, one unit of plait, usually long enough for an average wristband length. To make a longer plait you have to repeat all the stages over again as many times as necessary to give a 2,3,4,5-unit plait, etc. The slit lengths given above can be multiplied up to give a rough estimate for slit lengths in a belt length of similar width in the same thickness hide. If you want to change the width of the plait and the thickness of the leather, then do your own dummy run for a 1-unit plait length, and when you've worked out an appropriate slit length, multiply it up. If anything, cut the slits slightly short and do a trial plait – you can always lengthen the slits. If you cut them too long to begin with you'll either have to put up with a loose plait or extend the slits to accommodate another unit of plait.

Beadwork wristband

This wristband is a copy of an African bracelet we have – in fact the design and the colour scheme are pure Masai. We used a piece of 2·5–3mm-thick split cowhide as the base strap for the beadwork. You could use thin hide provided you can get an ordinary sharp needle through it easily. Cut the leather strap to fit your wrist and sew on the beads (instructions are given on page 66). Make the fastening from two lengths of rawhide thonging fixed with a tight bead (figure 141). Slide the bead up the thongs to tighten the bracelet.

Metalwork wristband

The shape and design of this wristband is shown in figure 142. Make up a thin cardboard pattern for whatever shape you decide on and draw round it in pencil on the leather (3mm-thick cowhide). Cut out the shape and add an edge groove. This can make a convenient boundary between two colours. Apply the two dyes carefully with a paintbrush, then dye and burnish the groove. Polish the wristband with saddle soap, and wax and burnish the edges.
Lastly decorate with eyelets, studs or rivets – we used eyelets and some silver strip. It was added in exactly the same way as the brass strip on the Green Belt on page 73.

Covered wristbands

For this type you need a good soft grain leather and a wooden or plastic bangle to cover. Some craft shops sell these specially for jewellery-making. We made two types (figures 143 and 144), the first covered with one complete piece of leather, the second wound with strips of leather.

1 (figure 143) Cut a strip of leather wide and long enough to completely cover the bangle (inside as well) with generous overlaps. Down the centre of the strip punch some lacing holes with a thonging chisel or slit punch and thread some lacing through them. Next smear the outside of the bangle with glue and wrap the leather round it but don't stick the ends down yet. Overlap the ends and use a Stanley knife to make a clean cut through both layers – remove the excess pieces so you're left with neatly abutted edges. Glue them down.

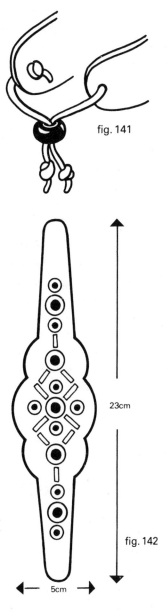

fig. 141

23cm

5cm

fig. 142

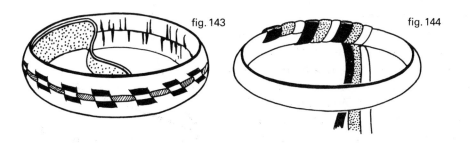

fig. 143   fig. 144

83

Now for the next part, which is a bit fiddly. Glue the edges of the leather to the inside of the bangle. Again let them overlap, then cut away the excess as before – you'll probably need something thinner than a Stanley to do this, e.g. a scalpel or small craft knife. The leather is bound to have wrinkles, so cut these off till you've made as neat and flat a finish as possible inside the bangle. To cover up all nasties, glue on a strip of leather to line the bangle. Then give the leather a good coat of saddle soap and rub well, especially along the edges of the lining to help smooth and flatten them.

2 The second type of bangle (figure 144) was made by winding three different coloured strips of soft leather over a wooden bangle. In fact you could do this over a large wooden curtain ring. Make sure the leathers are the same thickness and fairly thin. Cut the strips amply long enough – you don't want to join a strip halfway round.

Start the strips on the inside, as shown, and only glue as you go, because it'll take a bit of time getting the strips to lie with their edges evenly abutted. When you've gone right the way round, finish off the ends inside the bangle as best you can. They probably won't exactly meet the beginning of the strips, so just cut and glue them as neatly as possible to the inside so all the wood is covered. Coat the bangle with saddle soap and rub well, taking care not to push up the edges of the strips.

Moulded wristbands

If you wet sole leather it can be made to take up and hold a shape. We made the two bracelets shown on page 73 from 6mm-thick sole leather left over from making sandals. For the red and yellow coil type we cut a strip 46cm long and 1·5cm wide. For the other bangle cut the shape (figure 145) in thin card and use that as a template to draw cutting lines on the leather. Straight lines are easy to cut, curves are more difficult. On leather this thick there's nothing for it but to keep going over and over the initial cut until you're through. Bevel all edges, back and front.

Soften the leather in water for several minutes, then mould it round a jam jar or some other rigid object. Hold the leather in place with a piece of card wrapped around it and secured with sellotape or several large elastic bands. Because the leather is wet it picks up bruise marks easily – string or anything else wound around it will leave marks. The wide bangle was left undyed and the edge pattern

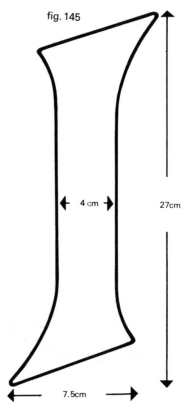

fig. 145

4 cm

27cm

7.5cm

burnt on after moulding with the flat tip of a soldering iron (see page 89). Then the edges were coloured and finished. The coil bangle was made as follows. Before moulding we cut grooves across the strip and dyed the various sections red and yellow. The grooves and edges were then dyed and burnished. When the dyes were thoroughly dry we soaked and moulded the leather. (Don't worry, leather dyes are usually fast.) After the bangle had dried out we dyed the inside of the coils and polished all surfaces with saddle soap.

Watch straps

These are really very simple to make. There are two basic designs. One requires a wide main strap (anything from 2 to 3mm-thick hide) and a narrower strap made from thinner leather which threads through the main strap, holds on the watch and makes the buckle strap. Alternatively the main strap can be made of thin leather, with a lining glued and stitched to the back. Use small straps and press studs to hold the watch on.

Belts

There are no tricky operations involved in making belts, especially the ordinary hide sort. On the other hand, they do reflect the amount of effort you put into them. In short, it pays to finish a belt well, and that means spending time on edges – bevelling and smoothing hide ones, lacing softer edges or perhaps turning them – and setting the buckle neatly.

We made five belts (page 73) expressly to show different ways of decorating and using the leather. Well, obviously this isn't a comprehensive collection, so in the next few pages we go into soft belts and covered ones and at the end of the chapter there are drawings and brief details of various other belt designs.

Leather For tough, hard-wearing belts use 3–4mm-thick tooling hide. This dyes, stamps, carves and plaits particularly well. Backs and shoulders are more rewarding to work with than bellies because they're denser and the edges are easier to finish. It may seem a bit thick and stiff at first but it soon softens up with wear. Thick but supple grain leathers lend themselves to rather different techniques (see Red Laced Belt, page 73). Any fine suede or grain leather can be used to make a soft belt. More expensive leathers like lizard, snake and ostrich, etc. are best used as a covering over a hide base (see 'Covered belts', page 88). On these softer belts you may need a lining. This can be skiver, other very fine leather or fabric.

Tools and equipment A Stanley knife, steel rule, edge beveller and a burnisher are musts for a hide belt. You'll also need rivets and their setting tools, a steel hammer, rotary or drive punch, plus a buckle or other hardware fastening (see pages 54–5). Depending on what style of belt you opt for you may need dyes, an edge groover, harness needles and waxed thread, plus tools for decorating. For soft leather belts you may well need leather shears for cutting them out, lacing for the edges (or glue if you turn them) and eyelets to reinforce the holes in the tongue.

Working order (The bulk of what follows applies to hide belts.)

1 Cut the belt blank, bearing in mind available buckle widths (see page 53). On the length allow a few extra centimetres at the buckle end plus whatever overlap you require on the tongue end. If anything, err on the generous side. We cut all our belts with a Stanley knife against a steel rule. Some craft shops sell pre-cut belt blanks, but at a price! You can also buy a special tool called a draw gauge for cutting strips, but the best of these is expensive and only worth it if you're going into belts in a big way. Remember the best belt lengths are cut from along the back of the hide (i.e. with the grain) where the leather is firm and even in texture. Belly strips sometimes won't dye quite so well, and the leather is less dense so the edges tend to fuzz and are hard to bevel and burnish properly.

2 Shape the tongue end. There aren't too many alternatives (figure 146a, b and c). Shape the buckle end if you like; usually we just clip the corners (figure 146c).

3 Bevel all edges, back and front.

4 Punch the holes in the tongue and make the buckle slot and rivet holes (see page 54). Cut an edge groove or crease if you want one. We're all in favour of them, as they give the edge a bit of emphasis on a plain belt and make a useful border around designs on a decorated one.

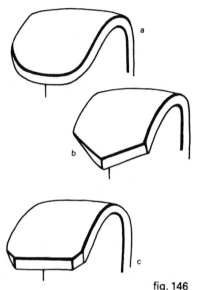

fig. 146

5 Do your decorating and dyeing or colouring (see Chapter 5). Darken the edge groove, if you've got one, with a felt tip pen (spirit-based), or with dye and a small paintbrush. Burnish along the groove with anything that looks as though it might do the job. The back of a knife works pretty well; we use the tip of a wooden pottery tool. Darken the edges (that includes the bevelled bits) using a felt tip, paintbrush and dye or, better still, glue a piece of felt into a firm roll and apply the dye with that (figure 147). Make sure the dye really penetrates the edges.

fig. 147

6 Give the belt a coat of saddle soap and rub beeswax into the edges. Then get going with the burnisher and rub, and rub, and rub till the edges are really smooth.

7 Fix on the buckle, and a keeper if necessary (see page 54).

A rugged belt of this sort is unlikely to need a lining except if you use the cutwork technique explained on page 68. The following two types of belt should have a lining.

Covered hide belts

If you want to make up a belt using a more exotic leather, say fine cape, pigskin, ostrich or reptile skin, then one way is to use a piece of hide as a stiffener, i.e. you cover the grain side of the hide with your special leather and finish the back of the belt with a lining.

Cut the hide to shape and bevel the front edges. Cut the special leather about 1·5cm larger all round than the hide and dampen it on the right side. Smear glue evenly all over the grain side of the hide and on the edges. Then lay on the special leather, smooth it well over the hide, pull it evenly round the edges and glue to the back of the hide. As the covering leather dries, it will shrink slightly and tighten over the hide.

If the covering leather is very thin, just flatten the turned edge with your mallet. If it looks like being a bit bulky, especially round curves or corners, carefully snip away any excess, then have a go with the mallet. To line the belt, cut a piece of skiver or other thin leather a little smaller than the finished belt size. Glue this lining to the back of the belt so that it hides the edges of the covering leather (figure 148). Stretch the lining slightly lengthways so it fits without wrinkling.

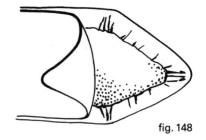

fig. 148

Soft belts

To make a soft belt cut a piece of fine leather about 1cm larger all round than the desired belt size, then turn over and glue the 1cm allowance. If you're using a thickish suede or grain split you may need to skive the edges before turning them. Cut Vs in the edge where necessary to facilitate turning.

As a lining you could use skiver, thin plastic or fabric. Turn and glue the edges of the lining just as you did for the soft leather, only make the finished lining a trifle smaller all round than the leather part. Lightly glue the lining in place just at the edges, then stitch all round (figure 149) – machine stitch if the thickness isn't prohibitive, otherwise saddle stitch with harness needles through pre-punched holes, or do a neat, close running stitch using a leather needle.

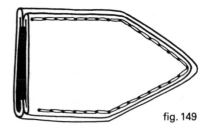

fig. 149

So much for belts in general, here are details of the belts shown on page 73.

Yellow belt

Judicious burning of leather can be quite a quick way of making monochrome designs. We did the branding on this belt with a cheap 25-watt electric soldering iron. This is a lightweight iron that takes a screw-in bit (a bit is the tip that you solder with and in this case do the burning with). Any DIY or tool shop should stock this kind of iron. By using the bit either on its edge or flat you can manage all sorts of lines and flourishes. We used the iron to draw lines against a steel rule – just like a pencil. The Ms (figure 150) were outlined with a thin line first, made with the edge of the bit, then 'shaded' in with the flat of the bit. The longer you leave the bit in contact with the leather the darker the burn. Don't do too large an area of really dark shading because the surface will crack if the leather is bent. Have some practice runs on scrap leather and work somewhere where you can have a window open, as the smell is nauseating.

For best results work on a good smooth piece of natural coloured hide. Dye afterwards, not before, and mark the design on the leather first with pencil.

The edge design on one of the moulded bangles (page 73) was produced just by using the bit flat on.

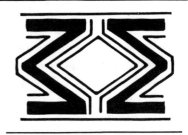

fig. 150

Green belt

On a finished belt length any of the usual metal hardware – rivets, eyelets and studs – make good decoration. On this belt (figure 151) we used some brass strip. Now, we happened to come across this in the recesses of a little craft shop, but to be honest it's not something you'll find that easy to get. However, you can buy silver strip. Some craft shops sell it and you should also be able to purchase it through a jewellery supplies merchant (look in your Yellow Pages). You may also find something you can use in a model-making shop. The Metalwork Wristband on page 73 illustrates a similar technique using silver strip and eyelets. If you do use metal strip, cut it into small lengths and bend these to make 'staples' (bend the ends at right angles in the jaws of flat-nosed pliers). Cut slits in the belt, poke the staples through, bend the ends over on the back with your fingers first, then flatten them gently with the mallet. Do this on a block of wood with several layers of fabric between the belt and the wood so the metal doesn't get marked on the right side. Line the belt with a strip of soft leather.

NB. We used a hinge instead of a buckle on this belt.

fig. 151

Brown cutwork belt

This technique – essentially it's reverse appliqué – produces a belt that looks as though it's been deeply carved. Two pieces of leather are needed – hide for the cutwork and a supple leather, a grain or flesh split about 1·5mm thick, to line the belt. This lining will need to be stuck and stitched to the hide, so before you start your design on the hide, mark the stitch line around the edge. Alternatively, cut an edge groove to take the stitching.

Use the Stanley knife to cut out small triangles, squares or diamonds in the hide. This is fairly fiddly to do and takes a bit of time, so if you're the impatient type and own a bag punch or large drive punch then maybe you could devise a design using these instead. Test all patterns on a small piece of hide first to see if your cut-outs allow the leather to bend evenly. Try not to overcut the corners; in fact it's best always to cut outwards from a corner. We completed our pattern with punched holes, and stamped circles (stamped with a piece of metal pipe). After dyeing we used a decorative stamp to make the pattern round the diamond cut-outs (figure 152).

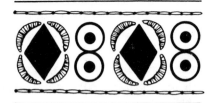

fig. 152

Colour the hide, taking care to darken the edges of the cut-outs (we use a black spirit-based felt tip for this). Leave the main edges for the moment.

Cut the lining leather a little wider than the hide. Spread glue on the back of the hide only, then stick on the lining strip stretching it well lengthways so it fits without wrinkling. Now stitch the two layers together all round and trim the lining flush with the hide edge. Re-glue any section where the layers have parted and pare off excess glue. Now bevel, colour and burnish the edges.

Belt ends

If you haven't got enough leather for an all-hide belt then you might consider just making the ends in hide. In this case the body of the belt is carpet webbing – a cheapie! At either end the webbing is glued between two pieces of hide – a front piece P which holds the buckle or makes the straps and a back piece Q (figure 153). After gluing, pound with the mallet to ensure adhesion and reduce bulk, then make stitch holes through the whole lot and saddle stitch. The stitching can be both structural and decorative.

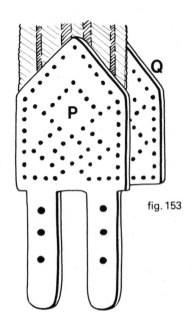

fig. 153

Red laced belt

Use a tough, flexible grain leather about 1·5mm thick. Cut a series of even slits along the middle of the belt about 2·5cm long and no more than 5mm apart. Twist the resulting strands as in figure 154a and thread lacing through to hold them in position. Extra laces, the dark ones in figure 154a, can be added through the strands top and bottom. By twisting the strands alternate ways you produce a different pattern (figure 154b).
Finish the belt edge with some type of lacing – we used Florentine lacing, see pages 42–3.

Other belt designs

Figure 155 shows some alternative designs for plain hide belts. Belt 155a is a simple affair that needs no hardware fastenings at all. Have a look at pages 81–2 for information on how to do a closed 3- or 5-strand plait. The method is just the same for a belt length (figure 155d). Alternatively, you might try your hand at carving a belt. All information on carving is given in Chapter 8.
Figure 156 shows some of the many ways of combining leather with other materials. In 156a, the metal rings (they could also be D-rings or rectangles) are joined by riveted loops of leather. This works out a bit heavy on rings, but if you can find a leathercraft supplier that'll sell them by the half hundred or so, the cost won't be devastating. Don't bother to calculate how much it'd cost if you bought them in little packets from haberdashery departments!
In 156b, pieces of thick hide are joined by thonging which runs through eyelets. Belt 156c is a variation on weaving leather (page 70), only here a continuous leather strip is woven through three lengths of thick cording. A chandlers (a yachting or sailing gear suppliers) is a good source for tough cording. You could use the cords to make tie ends for the belt, or pound them as flat as you can, then stitch and sew them between two pieces of leather and fix on a buckle as per normal.
Don't forget that most if not all of the decorating techniques mentioned in the first half of the book could be used on belt lengths.

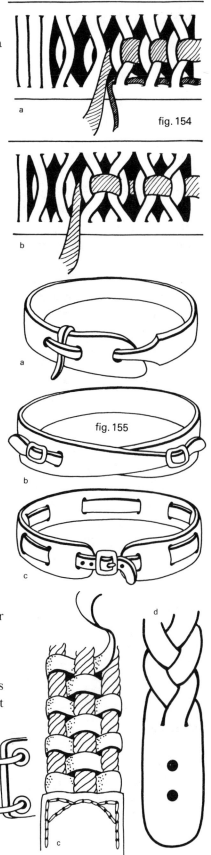

fig. 154

fig. 155

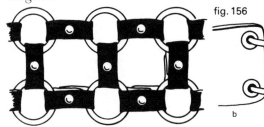

fig. 156

Wallets

Something flat with pockets which opens and shuts like a book – that's a wallet. There are literally thousands of variations on the theme, from pocket size bill folds to the table size folios which artists hump around. The wallet in the photograph on page 50 was designed to hold writing materials. Its actual size when closed is 38×28cm.

Leather Natural hide is about the most versatile of all leathers. The wallet on page 50 was made entirely of 2mm-thick natural vegetable tanned cowhide which we dyed and polished ourselves. For other remarks about wallet leather, look under 'Wallets in general', page 95.

Tools and equipment This type of project calls for a Stanley knife with a straight blade, a steel rule, a stitchmarker (or a plain old-fashioned ruler!), a mallet and round awl, an edge beveller, a skiving knife and a tool for incising the design on the cover (a groover, race or gouge). For stitching you'll need two harness needles and some strong thread.
Saddle soap is a must and so is a medium/dark dye if you want your incised design to appear lighter than the leather. If you reverse the idea (leave the leather undyed and use a dark stain or felt tip for the incised lines) the relief effect is almost entirely lost.

Construction This particular wallet is just two pieces of hide, S and T in figure 157, sandwiched together to form a main pocket and cover, with three smaller pockets stitched to the inside (S) and a double tongue and loop device to hold it shut. (This type of fastening is illustrated in figure 96, page 55.)

Cutting out First you cut two identical pieces of hide, one for the outer, the other for the inner cover. Then you cut a wide, round-cornered slot, the opening to the main pocket, in the centre of the inner cover (S). Now you cut out the inside pockets, plus a holding strap (U), a loop for the

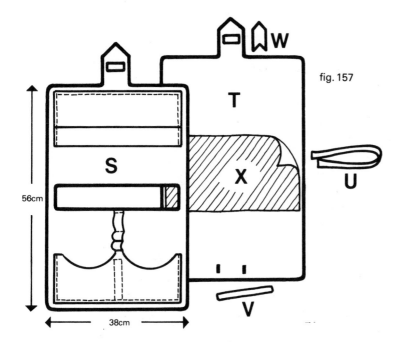

fig. 157

tongue to slot over (V) and a smaller tongue (W) to go through the loop. Remember to cut the slots in the main tongue and the two slots in X which take the loop V. Round off all the square corners and bevel all edges.

Cover design If you scrape away a dyed surface, the natural colour of the leather reappears. An edge groover is fine for making incised lines if you use it at such an angle that the heel doesn't bruise the leather. A freehand groover, race or gouge is even better but it must be sharp.
We began by cleaning the leather with white spirit, giving it several coats of diluted dye until the colour was even, and polishing it up with saddle soap. (Remember to dye all the little pieces as well, including the flesh side of the holding loop, and all the edges.) Then we traced the design onto the cover using tracing paper and a blunt pencil. Make shallow grooves to start with. When you have finished gouging, run something smooth – a spoon handle will do if you have no modelling tools – along each groove. Tone down the grooves with saddle soap, or with a light stain and then saddle soap. Polish vigorously.

Putting the pieces together Hide tends to look raw on the flesh side so we lined the opening of the main pocket with a piece of cape leather (X) – any stretchy leather will do. Stretch it as you glue it in place. That way it won't crease along the fold of the wallet.

Form the latch loop with a mallet, poke the skived ends through the slots in the outer cover and rivet them (figure 158).

fig. 158

Skive a little off the flesh side of the main tongue pieces (on S and T) to make them more flexible. Also skive the ends of the holding strap; this is sandwiched in the seam near the spine of the wallet. Slightly reducing the thickness of the pocket edges where they attach is also a good idea.

Stitching everything together comes last. Saddle stitch looks best. Sew the pockets to the inner cover first, and then the inner cover to the outer cover. Make your stitch holes, evenly spaced and in impeccable straight lines, with the round awl and mallet. You can stop the pockets jiggling about as you do this by lightly gluing their edges (not their free edges of course) to the leather underneath. Don't use sellotape as this will lift the polish. Remember to stitch the small tongue to the tongue of the outer cover (figure 159). Now, if you have a critical eye, you'll notice that a round awl makes smooth holes in the side you are working on, but rather nasty craters on the back, which doesn't matter a bit if the back is not on view. But if your stitching is going to be visible from both sides it's a pity to spoil one side with a row of craters. This is what happens if you put the inner and outer covers together and bang holes right through both thicknesses. So make your stitch holes round the edges of the inner and outer cover separately, both sets exactly matching. Tie off thread ends in between both thicknesses. Remember to include the holding strap in the edge seam. Another small point: it makes good sense to reinforce the seam at the top and bottom of the centre opening with extra stitching (figure 160).

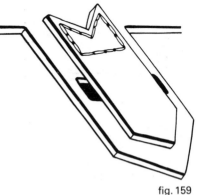

fig. 159

Gently and firmly fold the wallet in half, close the tongue and weight it down with lots of books for a day or two. Rub more saddle soap into the spine to keep it supple.

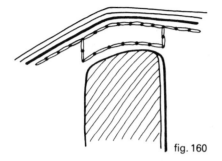

fig. 160

Wallets in general

Most follow this folding-main-pocket-plus-smaller-inside-pockets pattern. Thonging and lacing are often used instead of stitching, especially around outer edges (figure 161). Really it's much safer to stick with lighter-weight hide or firm dressed grain leather for wallets than trying to use some of the fine, soft leathers popular in the leather goods trade. First of all, they won't need lining or stiffening, and second, who wants to make too conventional a wallet? Inside pockets can be made of slightly thinner leather, but it must still be fairly stiff. Stretchy leathers are out. Pockets made of thin leather resist dog-earing better if they have turned or bound edges.

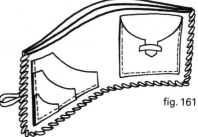

fig. 161

If you particularly want a soft pouchy-looking wallet, then nappa and all the softer leathers are fine for both cover and pockets. Outside edges can be firmed by binding or by turning and stitching (see Chapter 4).

Zips have a definite place in wallet-making. They look very professional on inside pockets (figure 162) and are easy to insert provided you put them in before you start sewing the pieces together. Just cut a square-ended slot the same length as the metal part of the zip and about 1cm wide. Centre the zip under the slot, glue it in place, make your stitch holes with a round awl and ply your needle. Saddle stitch or back stitch are equally strong.

Closures are a study in themselves. Clips, turnlocks, case locks and press studs are all possibilities, but we're prejudiced. We'd rather see a fastening made of leather – tongue and loop, loop and toggle or strap and buckle (see page 56). That said, some wallets need no closure. They fold shut and that's that.

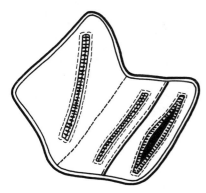

fig. 162

Bags

In this section we discuss four types of bag: the no-gusset bag (one or two main pieces), the one-gusset bag (see Shoulder Bag on page 52) and the two-gusset bag (three main pieces) and the box-type bag (one piece). A lot of the points we make are relevant to holdalls as well, which have a section of their own.

We have concentrated on shoulder bags, the sort with straps rather than handles, but if you read this section in conjunction with the chapters on handles and fastenings you'll gain a fairly comprehensive idea of the design possibilities open to you. Also, most of our comments apply to hide bags, because they're good subjects for dyeing, carving and stamping.

What you have to sort out is how you want your bag to look. You won't find any patterns as such here but you will find all the basic construction methods for hide bags, many of them applicable to other leathers, and lots of design ideas, which will enable you to make up your own patterns. Make a full-size mock-up of your ideas in felt or paper – don't waste too much time in miniature artist's impressions.

At the end of this section we give a 'general working order' which includes procedures relevant to all bags, with special reference to the gusseted type.

Leather We made our shoulder bag (page 52) from 3mm natural vegetable tanned cowhide. This thickness gives an averagely stout bag. Thinner hide, say 1·5–2mm, might require different edge treatment, e.g. laced or bound edges (see page 42). Thick hide, 3·5–4mm, lends itself to laced rather than stitched seams.

Tools You'll need a Stanley knife, steel rule, edge burnisher and beveller for sure. Probably you'll need a rotary or drive punch, rivets and their setting tools, harness needles and waxed thread (or lacing), a stitch marker, an awl or thonging chisel to make stitching or lacing holes, saddle soap and beeswax, and maybe dye as well. Depending on the style you may need a bag punch and

hardware fastenings for the shoulder strap and bag flap.
Tools for carving, stamping and designing on leather are
mentioned in Chapter 8.

No-gusset bag shapes

Nothing could be simpler than this. Almost any sort of
leather can be used, except very thick hide. Have a look at
pages 41–4 for ideas on edge joins for softer leathers.
Here are three useful designs: figure 163a is a bit like a two-
dimensional bucket – just two identical pieces of leather
joined together round the edges; figure 163b is a
conventional clutch purse, made from a single piece of
leather; figure 163c is virtually the same as 163a except that
it has flat hide handles (see pages 58–9 for other handle
suggestions).

One-gusset bag shapes

The three main pattern pieces are a back-and-flap, cut as
one piece, a front and a gusset (figure 164). These three
pieces are simply altered to make different-shaped bags.
The flap can be a full flap that echoes the shape of the bag, a
half flap, or some other shape altogether (figure 165).
For the sake of simplicity make the back and front of the bag
exactly the same shape and alter the width of the gusset to
make a fat or thin bag. The gusset can be the same width all
round or tapered towards the top of the bag.

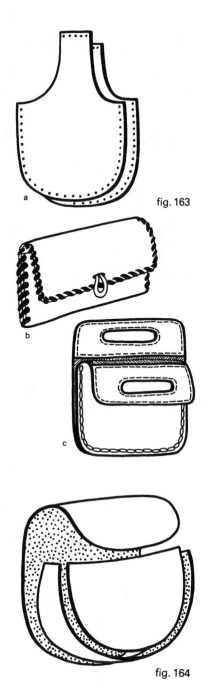

fig. 163

fig. 164

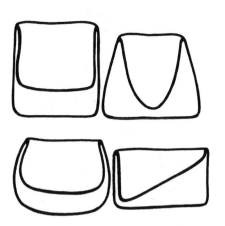

fig. 165

Two-gusset bag shapes

In this type the front, back and flap are continuous and it is the gusset shape which dictates the look of the bag (figure 166). Here are a few alternatives:

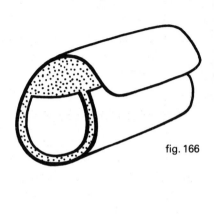

fig. 166

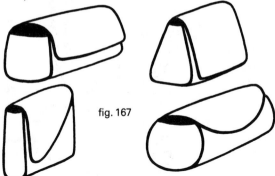

fig. 167

The flap can be shaped to suit the bag and type of fastening (figure 167).

Joining one- and two-gusset bags The gusset/s has to be sewn to the front and the back of the bag. There are three basic ways of joining gussets to bag fronts and backs – the method used depends to a certain extent on the thickness of your leather.

1 Use a plain seam with the leather joined wrong sides together (figure 168). We're going to refer to this as an 'outside seam'. This is suitable for hide up to about 3·5mm thick, the edges of which will bevel, stain and burnish to a good finish. If you use this type of seam on thin hide, either lace over the edges or bind them with soft leather (see Edges, page 41).

2 Use a plain seam with the leather joined right sides together (figure 169), an 'inside seam' – then turn the bag right side out. Obviously this is easiest to do with thin hide.

3 Join with an overlap seam (figure 170) that is either stitched (a) or laced (b). This method is suitable for medium thickness hide with good, firm edges, or for thick hide (up to 4mm).

Attaching straps to gussets One can avoid attaching straps altogether simply by extending the gusset/s to make a shoulder strap (figure 171). This takes fairly long strips of leather so you may have to cut single gussets in two halves and seam them together underneath the bag (skive the edges and use an overlapped seam). Alternatively extend

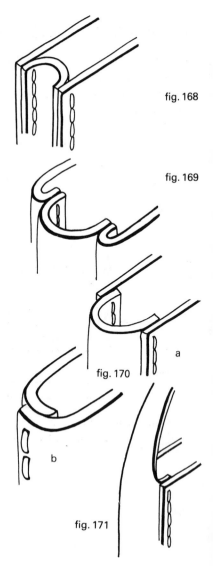

fig. 168

fig. 169

fig. 170

a

b

fig. 171

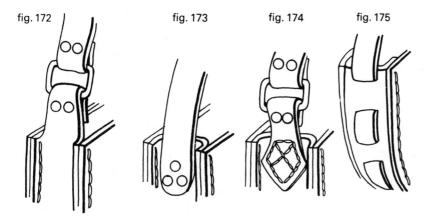

fig. 172   fig. 173   fig. 174   fig. 175

the gusset/s slightly and add separate strap lengths (figure 172). Otherwise add the straps directly to the top of the gusset/s (figure 173) or stitch on a separate tab to hold the straps (figure 174). All the joins can be either stitched, riveted or laced. You could also thread the straps through the gusset all the way round (figure 175).

Flap fastenings (see Fastenings, pages 55–6).

Pockets Most bags have an inside pocket of some kind. This can be made from thin hide or from softer leather and attached to the front or back of the bag inside. Here are two types:

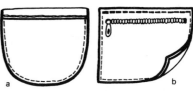

fig. 176

The top of 176a is turned or bound, otherwise it's sewn to the bag all round. It can echo the shape of the bag or be a completely different shape. To make the stitch holes, lightly sellotape the *right* side of the pocket to the *right* side of the bag, then make your holes through both thicknesses. This way there's a better chance of getting even-looking holes on the right side of the bag where the stitching shows. Type 176b is a 'free' pocket with a zip opening made from two pieces of leather joined together all round. This is attached with a line of stitching across the top.

Outside pockets could be made up in hide in either of the above ways – depending on their size they could be used on a shoulder bag or on a holdall.

Here are two other alternatives:

Cut a piece of thick hide as in figure 177a and on the flesh side cut two grooves close together along each fold line (this is only necessary on thick hide). Pound the folds with the mallet. Stitch the corners together and sew the pocket to the bag along the base first (right side to right side) then flip the pocket up and sew along the sides (figure 177b).

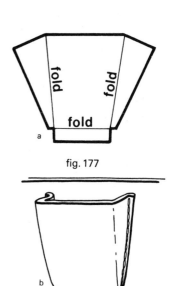

fig. 177

Your other alternative is to have a pocket with an all-round separate gusset, like half a mini one-gusset bag in fact (figure 178). Cut a groove all round to take the stitching. This will allow the gusset edges to bend so that the seam lies flat against the bag.

Either of these pockets could have a flap with a press stud or some other type of fastening (see pages 55–6).

Making a one-gusset bag pattern First of all decide on the shape, size and style of bag you want. It's no good trying to work out a pattern if you don't know exactly what you want to make. Assuming you have a pretty clear picture, draw the shape of the bag body full size on a large sheet of tracing paper. If it's to be curved, sketch one half of the curve, fold the paper in half and sketch the other half of the curve. Keep at it until you get the shape you want. You've now drawn the pattern for the bag front. Curve the top of the bag front very slightly (figure 179).

The bag front also gives you the shape for the back-and-flap piece. But before you draw out this second pattern piece you'll have to estimate how many centimetres you need across the top of the gusset – A in figure 180. If the finished width of the gusset (i.e. when it's sewn into the bag) is going to be 5cm, then allow that much extra in the back-and-flap piece. It's difficult to give a rule of thumb for this gusset allowance. What we've just said works if the gusset is reinforced by strap tabs so it stays fairly rigid and doesn't bulge inwards or outwards. But if the gusset is going to crease inwards at the top, as on a simple flap-over bag in thin hide without straps or handles, the gusset allowance in the back-and-flap piece would have to be considerably less. So, to draw up the full back-and-flap pattern, start by marking a long straight line in the centre of your tracing paper. This is a centre line running the length of the back-and-flap. Trace the bag front pattern onto it, aligning the fold in the bag front with the centre line you've just drawn. Add the gusset allowance along the top, then trace off the bag front shape again. Now curve the edges of the gusset allowance slightly inwards (this is to allow the handles free passage), and, *voilà*, you have the shape of the back-and-flap piece (figure 181). Now's the time to alter the shape of the flap if you want to.

The gusset can be completely straight, or taper towards the ends, as for our bag (figure 181). Whether it's straight or tapered it's as well to make a pattern piece for it (useful when you're trying to decide the best way to cut your

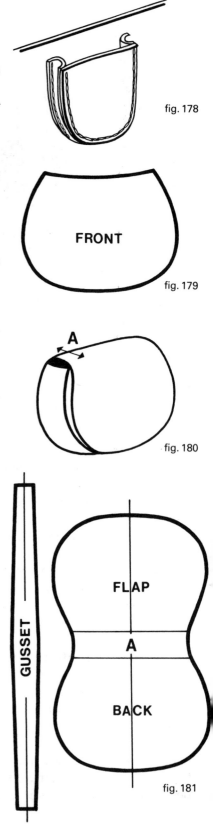

fig. 178

FRONT

fig. 179

A

fig. 180

GUSSET

FLAP

A

BACK

fig. 181

pattern pieces out of your leather). Calculate the approximate length of the gusset by measuring round the bag front pattern with a piece of string. Make your gusset pattern a trifle longer than necessary – you'll work out the exact length it needs to be when you come to make the stitch holes in the *leather* gusset. If you're drawing a pattern for a tapered gusset, again work from a centre line (figure 181). Widths for the tops of gussets usually range from 4 to 9cm. Cut pattern pieces for strap tabs and fastenings, if any. When you're satisfied with your pattern (do a trial run in felt if you're really dubious) cut it out accurately in thin card. Lay the pieces of card on your hide and juggle them round to capitalize on the prime parts of the leather. Back and shoulder areas are best. Draw round the pattern pieces in pencil and – now for the most nerve-racking part – cut them out.

Making a two-gusset bag pattern This is probably simpler to work out than the one-gusset type. The all-in-one front/back/flap piece will be roughly rectangular with one end shaped to make the flap and the other slightly curved to make the top of the front. The length of this piece depends on the shape of the gussets, so work out your gusset shape first, using the folding in half and tracing method to get a symmetrical shape. Measure round the gusset with string to find out how long the front/back needs to be and add on a suitable amount for the gusset allowance and flap.

Making stitch holes It's very important that the stitch holes (or lace holes for that matter) in the gusset and the bag front and back match up. Here's how you go about it. Run a stitchmarker round the edge of the bag front about 5mm in from the edge. Now tot up the number of marks you've made. If your bag has a straight gusset run off a corresponding number of marks along one edge. If it's a tapered gusset there's a little more to it. Find the exact centre of the gusset and mark it with a pencil dot. If the number of stitch marks on the bag front was odd, count the centre dot on the gusset as one stitch mark and run off half the number on either side. If the number was even, start half a stitch length either side of the centre dot. Repeat the operation to make the stitch marks for the bag back. Check that you've got the right number of stitch marks. Make the stitch holes with an awl or thonging chisel working on the right side of the leather. Now you can cut the gusset to the correct length. Follow exactly the same procedure for making lace holes or slits.

Just one thing, if your leather is very thick and you want to use an outside seam, it helps to cut edge grooves in the gusset to take the stitching. This allows the gusset seams to bend slightly so the back and front of the bag remain flat, as in figure 168.

Make stitch holes for tabs by sellotaping them lightly in place on their respective backings and making the holes through both thicknesses at once.

Attaching gussets If you intend to stitch your seams, use saddle stitch (see figure 51, page 37). It's very strong and looks very professional. Count the same number of holes, say four or five, from the top on each piece (gusset and bag front or back) and start stitching. Stitch to the top of the seam, cross over the top of the edge and continue down through the holes you've just stitched through (figure 182) and on round the seam. Do the same double stitching when you reach the top the other side. This reinforces the seam at its most vulnerable points and saves you having to tie off the thread in a conspicuous place.

We prefer to start lacing at the top of gusset seams. Lace over the top edge and twice through the first hole (figure 183). The lace end lies between the two thicknesses. Any of the edge lacing techniques illustrated on pages 42–3 would be suitable for attaching gussets.

Box-type bag

This type of bag is pretty simple to put together. It looks nice and chunky if you use good thick leather. Scaled down and made of thinner hide it makes an excellent belt purse. It's up to you whether the bag ends up really boxy with creased corners (figure 184) or semi-boxy with rounder corners (figure 185). You also have a choice between completely overlapped side tabs, perhaps with two lines of lacing (figure 186), or tabs that overlap just to accommodate a single line of lacing. Incidentally lacing isn't compulsory. You could stitch, but lacing is easier and gives the bag more character.

The pattern sketched here makes up into a longish flat bag with tabs that overlap by about 2cm (figure 187). Try this pattern out in paper to see if it's what you want. If not, alter the dimensions to make it fatter, wider, taller or much smaller, with or without completely overlapped side tabs. The pattern can be cut as one piece, but if this proves wasteful or impossible given the size of your leather, cut and

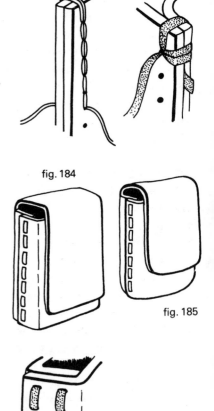

fig. 182   fig. 183

fig. 184

fig. 185

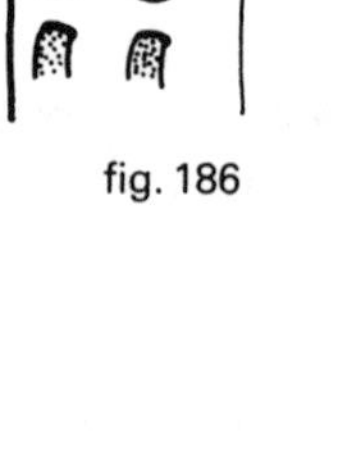

fig. 186

add the flap separately. Make sure all the angles are true right angles.

Bevel all edges, then mark an even number of slots (or holes) down one side flap. Duplicate them exactly on the other three side flaps. Cut the slots. To make sure you position the slots in the bottom flaps accurately, fold the bag up and mark the positions through the slots in the side flaps. Punch these slots. Then cut shoulder straps plus any tabs needed for the flap fastening. If you're making a belt purse cut two leather strips for holding the purse to the belt (figure 188), and make two pairs of slots in the back of the bag for them to thread through. After dyeing but before assembling the bag, poke the strips through the slots and join their skived ends with small rivets.

Dye all the pieces and finish the edges. If you want well-defined corners, cut two grooves close together in the flesh side of the leather along each fold line. Fold the leather and gently tap along the folds with a mallet. Cut some lacing strips and lace the sides together starting at the bottom of each side. Secure the lace end with a small rivet through the bottom of the bag (figure 189). Lace through the slots to the top of the sides then thread the end back through the previous lacing and pull tight. Include the strap ends in the last two or three 'stitches'.

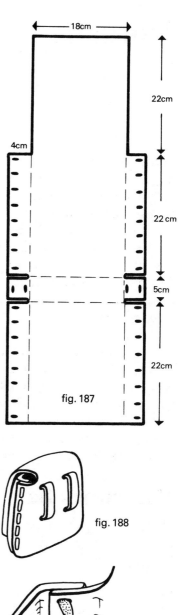

fig. 187

General working order

1 Cut out all your pattern pieces in leather.

2 Bevel edges where necessary (e.g. bag back, front, flap, shoulder straps and tabs). Don't bevel the edges of the front, back and gusset on the flesh side if you want outside seams (page 98). Go ahead and bevel the flesh side if you're using overlap seams.

3 Make all stitch holes, lace holes and slots.

4 Dye all your bits and pieces and give them a coat of saddle soap. For an outside seam bag, wax and burnish the top edges of the bag front, the edge of the flap, the gusset ends, and all strap and tab edges. Leave the gusset sides and the edges of the front and back for the moment. For an overlap seam bag finish all edges at this stage.

5 Sew or rivet on all tabs, fastenings and pockets.

6 Sew or lace the gusset/s to the rest of the bag.

7 If you've opted for an outside seam, wax and burnish the combined gusset/front/back edges.

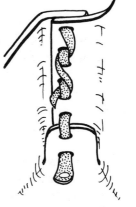

fig. 188

fig. 189

Holdalls

Making a holdall is not essentially different from making a bag, except that one tends to use leather other than hide to reduce weight. Both the Patchwork Bag and the Carpet Bag (photographs on page 51) are two-gusset bags, one of four types of bag discussed in the previous section. They illustrate various ways of using softer leathers and could easily be scaled down to handbag size.

Temporarily we've extended the meaning of holdall – 'holds all your North Pole equipment', 'holds all your dirty laundry' – to cover the Carrying Straps photographed on page 51.

It's worth making the point here that although one doesn't want a holdall to be too heavy, it needs a certain amount of body. This means using thin leathers with a backing of some kind (canvas, denim), or 'bag hide' (flexible vegetable-tanned cowhide split to a thickness of 1·5–2mm) or fairly thick but supple chrome-tanned cowhide. Flesh splits, however thick, never keep their looks as grain leather does.

Patchwork Bag

Hints on patchwork appear on page 67. Where it is attached to the zip and the gussets the patchwork is turned for extra strength.

Leather For the patches we used scraps of shoe upper leather, but almost any grain leather 1·25–1·5mm thick would do. Thick denim provided the extra stiffness and body we wanted for the main part of the bag. The gussets were made of 2mm-thick chrome-tanned cowhide and the handles of nappa, though any soft grain leather about 1mm thick would do.

Tools and equipment Leather shears, a Stanley knife, a round awl and mallet for making stitch holes, and some stitching implements – a sewing awl, or a couple of harness needles, and a sewing machine – are really all that is wanted in the way of tools. Other sundries needed are glue, waxed thread, a heavy duty zip, a piece of hardboard to stiffen the bag bottom inside and four domed studs to prevent the base getting scuffed.

Working order

1 Make a panel of patchwork somewhat bigger all round than the measurements given in figure 190. A panel this big may pose manoeuvring problems if you're joining your patchwork by machine, in which case make it in two halves and join them together with an abutted seam, with a leather backing strip on the outside as well as the inside.

2 Trim the patchwork to the dimensions shown in figure 190. Glue the long edges under by 1·5cm and pound them with a mallet to flatten them.

3 Cut out the gussets – they're just 24cm squares with their corners rounded off. Make the same number of stitch holes round each (5mm is a good distance from the edge), working from the mid-point of the bottom edge to within 5cm of the mid-point of the top edge (figure 191). Make the same number of holes along the long edges of the patchwork panel, again working from the mid-point of each edge. Turn the short edges of the patchwork under 4·5cm from the last stitch hole, and glue and flatten them (you may have to trim off a centimetre or two because you really only need a turn-under of about 1·5cm). This means there will be a gap left for the zip. From the inside, the top corners of the patchwork panel should now look like figure 192.

4 Now insert the zip. Glue it in place before you make stitch holes. It's also a good idea to do a few tacking stitches so that you don't wrench the leather away from the zip as you manipulate your needles in and out of the bag, which is now an open-ended tube. It's marginally easier if you start your stitching in the middle of the zip and work out towards the ends. Glue and sew pull tabs to the zip at each end (figure 193).

5 Next come the handles, easier to attach with the bag in this open-ended state than complete with gussets. Decide where you want the handles to sprout from – near the top of the sides is structurally best. We used rolled handles, as in figure 111, page 58, attached with tabs of thickish leather (the same as that used for the gussets) inside and outside, stitching through all thicknesses. Bang the ends of the handles well to splay and flatten them.

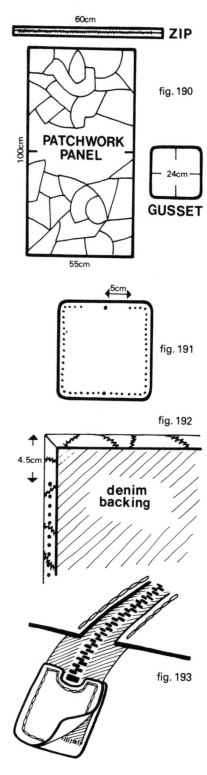

60cm

ZIP

PATCHWORK PANEL

fig. 190

100cm

24cm

GUSSET

55cm

5cm

fig. 191

fig. 192

4.5cm

denim backing

fig. 193

6 All that remains is to sew the gussets in place – a piece of cake! Your stitch holes are ready and waiting. Double stitch through the first few holes at the top of the gusset for extra strength. Finally glue a piece of hardboard – it needs to be about 50×15cm – to the bottom of the bag inside, and bang the four domed studs through from the outside.

Carpet Bag

This is a two-gusset bag, one of the four types discussed on pages 97–102. Figure 194 is a guide to the size and shape of pattern we used, but if you fancy something smaller, fatter, or taller, then draw the shape of gusset you want (it's this that determines the overall shape of the bag) and measure round it to estimate the length required for the main bag piece.

Leather We used three sorts for this bag: 1mm-thick split cowhide (though any firm grain leather would do) for the panels that bind the top of the bag, the edge binding, the lacing and the small plaits; very soft, thin leather – cape scraps actually – for binding the tops of the gussets and lining the strap slits; and 3mm-thick natural vegetable tanned cowhide for the straps.

Tools and equipment You'll need a Stanley knife and steel rule, leather shears or sharp scissors, a rotary punch, a lacing needle, glue and dye, harness and leather needles, with strong waxed thread.
We happened to have a piece of old carpet so we used that for the main bag piece and gussets, but you could use leather, a piece of thick tapestry fabric, canvas or even chunky corduroy instead. If you do use carpet, steer clear of anything with a pile – it just makes the going more difficult. If you use a fabric, glue some stiff canvas or denim to the back of it just to give it body. Do this before you cut out the pattern. You also need a piece of hardboard or stiff cardboard to reinforce the bottom of the bag inside.

Working order

1 Cut the gussets and main bag piece in carpet (figure 194). Cut two pieces of firm leather to bind the top edges. Glue them over the carpet and hand stitch along the shaped edge (figure 195). We added a small plait in the same leather to

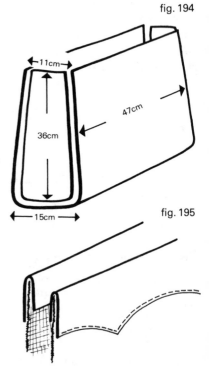

fig. 194

fig. 195

cover this stitching and decorate the edge. Hand stitch it on so the thread is hidden in the plait. Bind the top of each gusset with a piece of the softer leather.

2 Cut and make up the strap handles (figure 196). We made these in four sections – two wide bottom pieces that give the base of the bag extra support, and two plaited handle sections. (See pages 41–2 for finishing plain hide edges, and pages 81–2 for closed-end plaits.) On our bag the straps are held together on the inside of the bag by sets of large press studs so that you can get the handles inside the bag and so that the handles are adjustable.

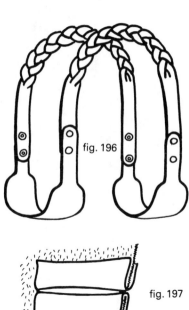

fig. 196

If you want handles that go right round the bag on the outside, make up similar strap sections and sew or rivet them to the main bag piece now. NB. This method cuts out all of stage 3.

3 If you decide to have the handles disappear inside the bag you'll need to make slits in the main bag piece. Note the general position for these in the photograph on page 51. Where the slits are made in the carpet section you'll need to line the slit edges rather like buttonholes. Glue two little pieces of the thin leather round the lips of the slit (figure 197). Then cut a piece of the firm leather (with a slot in it) to cover the front of the slit. Glue it in position and stitch round the slot (figure 198). We added a small piece of plaiting above the slot (figure 199), the ends of which were poked through slits to the back of the carpet where they were glued and stitched down. Line the back of the slit with a piece of firm leather. This can just be glued on (figure 200).

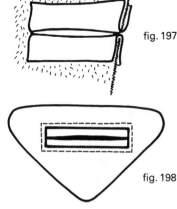

fig. 197

fig. 198

Where the straps emerge through the slits in the leather-covered top edges, just bind the lips of the slits with pieces of the firm leather. Add a little plait below the slit if you like and line the back of the slit as before.

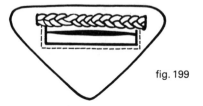

fig. 199

4 Now you're ready to put the bag together. Stitch in the gussets (wrong sides together) using thick thread to cross-stitch over the edges. Stop the stitching about 4cm down from the top corners (figure 201). You'll see why in a minute.

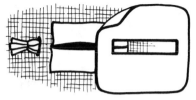

fig. 200

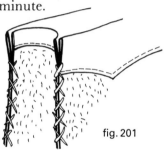

fig. 201

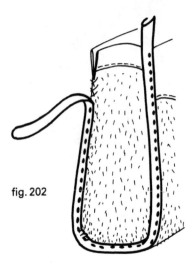

fig. 202

5 Cut some edge binding strip from the firm leather (wider than you need) and glue it lightly round the seams; but don't stick the edges of it down. Leave a few centimetres of spare binding at each top corner. Make lacing holes in the edges with the rotary punch through all layers (figure 202). Now trim the binding leather to within an even distance of the holes all round.

At the top of each corner turn the extra binding over the top to the inside of the bag, gluing and creasing it snugly into the seam – this is why you didn't stitch right to the top. Now re-punch the lacing holes on these sections (figure 203).

6 Lace all round the bag, through every other hole first, then back through all the remaining holes. Take the lacing over the top of each corner (figure 204).

7 Thread through the handle sections and do up the press studs.

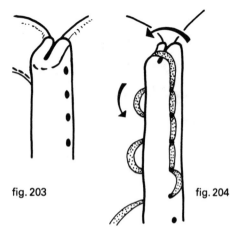

fig. 203

fig. 204

Carrying straps

These are ideal for carrying round lumber like sleeping rolls, beach gear, dirty washing, etc. They consist of a saddle-shaped piece of hide, a couple of long straps and a flat handle (figure 205). The information on making a handle of this sort is covered on page 57. The straps are essentially belt-like, so flick through the Belts section for the salient points on making.

Leather The whole contraption is made from 3mm-thick natural vegetable tanned cowhide.

Tools and equipment You'll definitely need a Stanley knife with straight and curved blades, a steel rule, a skiving knife, rotary punch, an edge beveller, mallet, rivets and their setting tools, an awl for making stitch holes, harness needles and strong waxed thread, a burnisher, beeswax and saddle soap, and two buckles. If you copy our design you'll also need an edge groover, stamps for decorating (we just used the two home-made types shown on page 30), leather paints and dye.

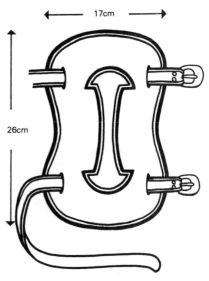

fig. 205

Working order

1 Make up a cardboard pattern for the saddle part. Draw round this on the grain side of the leather to give a cutting line. Cut out the saddle, straps and handle parts (see hints on cutting curves, on page 23).

2 Bevel all edges and add edge grooves if you want them round the saddle, along the straps and on part 1 of the handle. Cut the four strap slots in the saddle. Either use a bag punch for this or, if you're without one, use the method suggested on page 54, figure 88. Dampen the leather and stamp the pattern round the saddle edges.

3 Dye all pieces, then darken all the edges, slot edges and grooves with dye and a paintbrush or with a spirit-based felt tip. Burnish the grooves well. Colour the stamped pattern with leather paints. Wax all edges and burnish them well. Polish all pieces with saddle soap.

4 Make up the handle and stitch it to the saddle. Fix the buckles on the straps and thread them through the slots.

Moccasins

North American footwear is a fascinating subject.
'Moccasin' is an Iroquois word which willy-nilly got
applied to the footwear of every other tribal group. Very
broadly speaking there are, or were, two basic moccasin
types, the centre seam type and the side seam type (figure
206a and b). Some tribes, the Assiniboine and the Kiowa
Apaches, found a hard sole necessary but most used the
same leather – buffalo hide – for uppers and soles.
In this chapter we'll be telling you how to make your own
version of the moccasin pattern in figure 209 (this was the
pattern used for the moccasins in the photograph, page 76)
and how to put it together. Other designs are not radically
different – most include a gathered toe, turndown flap, heel
tab and thong tie.

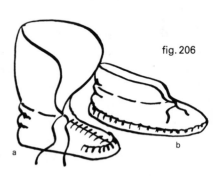

fig. 206

Leather What you're looking for here is softness and a
thickness of 1·5–1·75mm. Everyone thinks of moccasins as
fuzzy, not smooth. This is because traditionally moccasin
leather was unhaired by scraping, which left the grain side
rough. Since you're unlikely to come across the genuine
article here's what to look for instead: very soft, chrome-
tanned cowhide 1·5–1·75mm thick (in which case you
would use the sueded side as the right side); very thick and
firm cowhide split; thinner flesh splits used double
thickness, or thinner grain splits used double thickness
(with the suede sides outside). The last two suggestions are
unorthodox, but they work.
Your feet are certainly tenderer than a Sioux warrior's, so
you'll need a sole of some sort. Thick tooling hide, plus or
minus a stick-on sole, is good enough really – no desperate
need for sole leather. Aim at a finished sole thickness of
about 6mm. Glue two thicknesses of hide together if need be
or make up the thickness with a non-leather sole (see note
on non-leather soling, page 118).

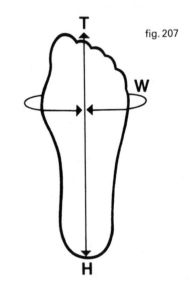

fig. 207

Tools and equipment The essentials here are leather
shears, a round awl and mallet, harness needles and an edge
groover, plus of course glue, beeswax, waxed linen thread,
some hide thonging and a tape measure.

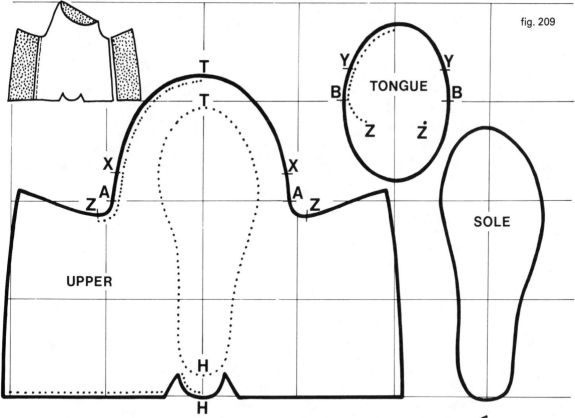

fig. 209

Making a moccasin pattern The vital measurements to take are these: toe to heel, which we'll call TH, and round the widest part of your foot, W (figure 207). TH will be the length of the sole and W will be the finished measurement of the toe at its widest point (figure 208).

Figure 209 is the pattern we used for the moccasins in the photograph. All the proportions are accurate – we've given grid squares to scale it up to your foot size.

AA and BB should add up to W plus 5mm; this 5mm allows for seams and is on the stingy side because moccasins stretch with wear.

$$AA + BB = W + 5mm$$

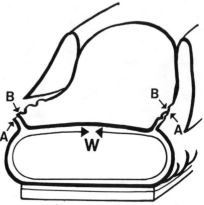

fig. 208

Look at the pattern again. The distance between TT should be the distance between the tip of your sole and the base of your big toe nail, about 3cm in the average adult. HH needs to be about 2cm.

To make a pattern which fits you, draw yourself a nice rounded sole shape round a tracing of your foot and transfer it to a large sheet of paper. Draw in the line TH. Draw another line slightly more than two-fifths of the way down

111

TH crossing it at right angles. Your two As will lie along this line. Now, how wide at its widest point do you want the tongue of the moccasin? Probably between 6·5 and 9cm. Subtract this from your W + 5mm measurement to get your correct AA measurement. Now try to draw a pattern of similar proportions to that above, remembering our observations about TT and HH.

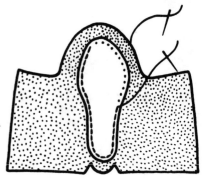

Note that the tongue is symmetrical but that the toe piece of the upper isn't. It follows the line of the sole and is a bit more generous on the instep side as it curves round into the flap.

As usual with anything that has to fit reasonably well it pays to do a trial run in felt before you launch into leather. Make a final corrected pattern in thin card.

NB. The type of pattern discussed here needs one important alteration if you plan to use single thickness grain leather with the suede side out. To overcome the problem of having flaps with the grain side showing cut the flaps separately and sew them on to the rest of the upper as shown at top left in figure 209.

fig. 210

Cutting out If you're using double thickness leather glue it together to make the double thickness before you do any cutting. Spread glue sparingly and evenly over the whole of one of the surfaces. Use shears to cut out the uppers and tongues, and shears or a curved Stanley to cut your soles.

Making stitch holes It saves a lot of trouble if you make all your stitch holes while your leather is flat. Three sets of holes are needed: one set to attach the soles to the uppers, another for the back seams of the uppers, and another to join the uppers to the tongues. And you sew them in that order.

Attaching soles to uppers First you need to prepare your soles, using the grain side of your hide on the bottom. (If you are using two or even three thicknesses of hide, roughen up all the surfaces to be glued with coarse glasspaper or a stiff wire brush, knock off the loose particles and glue them together. Pound with a mallet so that the glue penetrates all the cracks.) Beeswax and burnish the edges, then use an edge groover to cut a groove all round the bottoms (about 5mm from the edge is about right). This will take the stitching, i.e. a recessed seam (figure 42, page 35).

Now glue each sole to the underside of the upper which belongs to it. Get out your mallet and round awl, and bang an evenly spaced set of stitch holes round each groove and through all thicknesses. Next, you wield a pair of harness needles and waxed linen thread, and saddle stitch soles and uppers together (figure 210).

If you plan to add an extra layer of non-leather soling, now is the time to do it while your moccasins are still flat. Roughen up the leather and non-leather surfaces, glue them together, and pound with a mallet.

Back seams We butted the edges of the backs together with cross stitch.

Now come the heel tabs (figure 211). Make the same number of holes in the moccasin back and heel tab. Gather the latter slightly so that it curls up to meet the back. Stitching (saddle stitch again) in this area is a bit fiddly, but persevere.

Toe/tongue seam A good-looking way of attaching the gathered part of the toe to the tongue is to make, say, 18 triple sets of holes between XX and 18 single holes between YY (figure 212). The toe is then gathered between XX, leaving the middle hole of each threesome unthreaded. When the gathering thread is pulled tight the unthreaded holes line up opposite the holes in the tongue, ready to be oversewn. There are the same number of holes between XZ and YZ. Figure 213 shows the kind of arrangement we're talking about. Note that the oversewing stops at the AB point and continues to Z as saddle stitching (figure 214).

Finishing To hold the top of the moccasins snug round the foot, thread some lengths of thonging through the top of the turned-down flaps. (You'll see what we mean from the photograph, page 76.) Soften the thonging first with neatsfoot oil or saddle soap. The thongs only pop through to the inside for short bursts – this stops them chafing. Skive the ends of the thongs thin enough to poke through a bead or two. Push the ends, smeared with a little glue, back into the bead hole.

Moccasins tend to have a lot of personality. Those in the photograph strongly resisted any decoration. We considered fringes, beadwork, lacing, etc. but in the end decided they looked better plain.

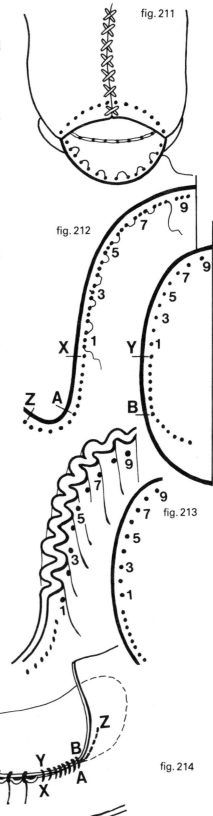

fig. 211

fig. 212

fig. 213

fig. 214

Sandals

This chapter starts with hints on how to design your own sandals, takes you through the making step by step, and ends with comments on the sandals photographed on page 76. Most sandals are put together as in figure 215.
The extensions of the upper get sandwiched between the sole and topsole. What bonds the sole to the topsole? Neoprene glue, a lot of pounding with a hammer and for extra insurance several nails banged strategically through all thicknesses.

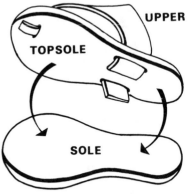

fig. 215

Leather For the sole you need 9–12 iron sole leather (between 5 and 6mm thick). A fore end or range, just over 1ft², is the smallest quantity you can buy. That represents one pair of man-size soles. You can make bangles (page 83) out of the scraps.
Topsoles don't need to be quite as tough but they need to be near the thick end of the natural vegetable tanned cowhide range, between 3 and 4mm thick if possible. Latigo is good if you can get it, otherwise use liberally saddle-soaped tooling hide.
And the uppers? Well, how tough are your feet? You want leather that will take the shape of your foot without chewing or chafing, but it must stand up to stress and tearing strains. For fairly stout uppers we suggest really flexible vegetable tanned cowhide about 2 to 2·5mm thick, or latigo, which is softer and waxier, of a similar thickness. Otherwise try to get hold of any leather specifically made for shoe uppers (calf, pigskin, glacé kid, 'side teather' or split cowhide finished as shoe leather) and give it a skiver lining. Finished thickness, upper leather plus lining, should be in the region of 2mm.

Tools and equipment Number one in the tool line is a Stanley knife with a curved blade for cutting soles. You'll also need a steel hammer and a last, or a hunk of metal that will do as a last (see page 25), coarse and fine glasspaper and something hard and smooth for burnishing sole edges. And you may need shears and a straight-bladed Stanley as well. Any stitching will require an awl and harness needles. Neoprene glue is a must; cobblers' nails are optional, as you will see.

Making a sole pattern Stand on a piece of paper, in bare feet, and draw round one foot with a pencil held vertically. Now simplify and stylize your pencilled outline. Figure 216 shows some of the commonest sole shapes.
Do you want a little or a lot of sole showing? A bit extra all round could give you scope for decorative stamping or stitching. When you've got a shape that satisfies you, make a template of it in thin card.

Designing the uppers Uppers are very personal. Maybe you don't feel safe without ankle straps. Maybe toe rings or thongs between the toes are out because you always wear socks. Whatever your predilections remember that an upper is no good unless it keeps the sole exactly under your foot.
Sandals a, b, c and d in figure 217 will 'walk' better than e because they hold the foot against the sole at two points, toe and instep, instead of one. Adding ankle straps makes any sandal easier to keep on. Figure 218 shows some of the commonest styles.

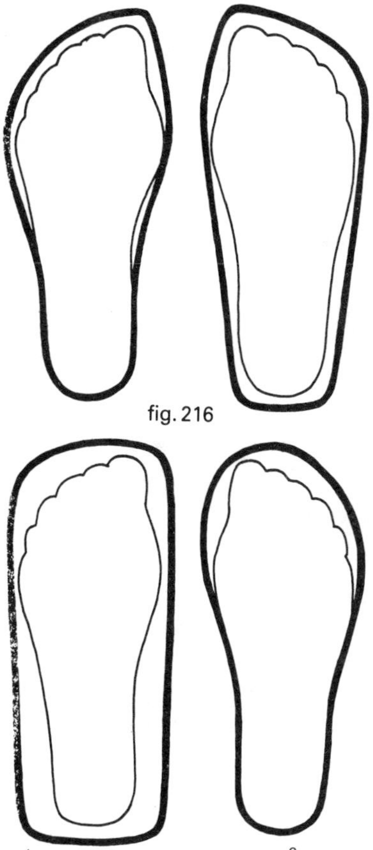

fig. 216

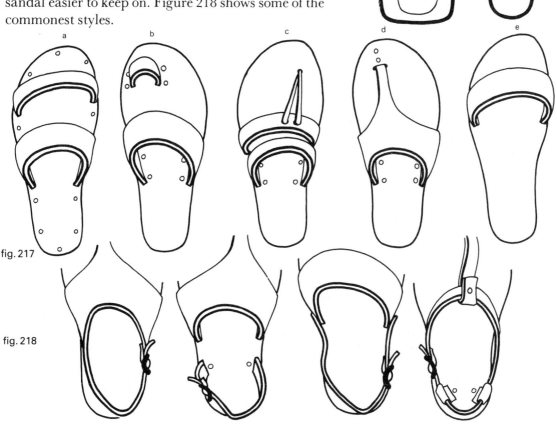

fig. 217

fig. 218

Personally we like one-piece uppers. Before they were attached to the topsoles the uppers of the sandals photographed on page 76 looked like figure 219. This was the pattern that fitted a friend's foot – it would have to be altered to fit yours. We've indicated how the pattern can be extended to make ankle straps or do away with the strap between the toes. The tassels and the appliquéd cutwork are just decoration.

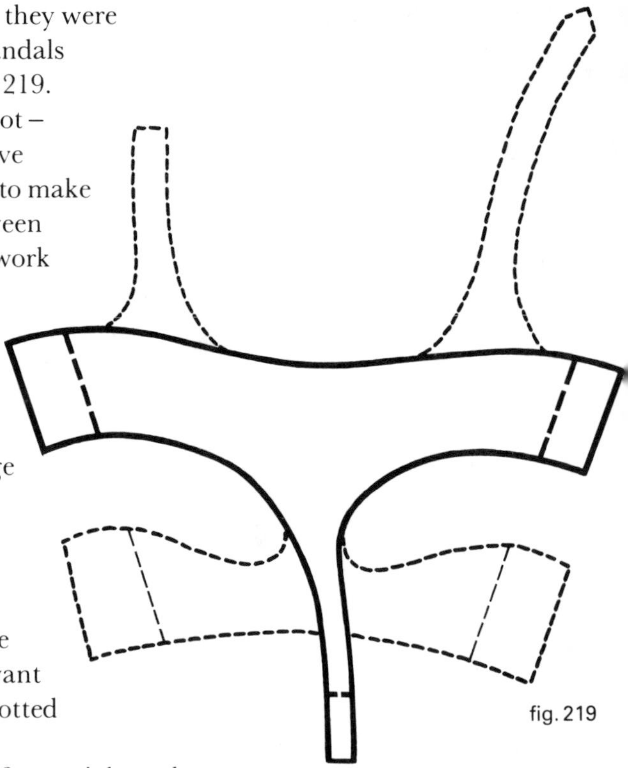

The best guarantee against a sandal slipping fore and aft or sideways is a snug band or strap around the instep, attached the same distance from your heel on either side. Resist your quite natural urge to attach it farther forward on the inside of the foot (figure 220).

Never make between-toe straps narrower than 6mm and allow plenty of spare for buckle attachments. If your straps cross one another at any point, decide whether you want them sewn or riveted at that point or just slotted through each other.

So, back to your foot again. Take a piece of material – pale-coloured felt is very good – and wrap it round your foot. Use sellotape to keep it in place. Now place your wrapped foot on top of your sole pattern. You're going to draw on the material, in biro, the shape of upper you want.

Mark where your intended straps meet the sole. All straps designed to meet the outer edge of the sole should in fact meet it 5mm or more inside it, so make allowance for this. Use a strip or strips of material to work out the shape and lie of any ankle straps.

Cut out the shapes you have just drawn, allowing an extra 3cm on the ends of all straps which attach to the sole; this is the extra which gets sandwiched between the sole and topsole. Fit the shape on your foot again. Fiddle and fuss until it really fits – it's worth it.

Finally, make a template of your design, marking on it any strap crossing points and also the points where the upper will slot through the topsole. Go back to your sole template and mark and cut out these slots. They should follow the curve of the sole edge and be at least 5mm away from it.

fig. 219

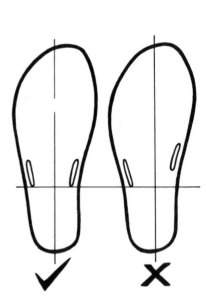

fig. 220

116

Cutting out You've a left foot and a right foot! So flip your
sole template over to draw your second sole. Use it to draw
a left and right topsole as well. Cut your slots in the topsoles
only – make them a shade wider than the thickness of the
leather you're using for the uppers. Cut the slots with a
Stanley knife and smarten up the ends with a hole punch if
you have one.

Brutality doesn't pay when cutting soles – you're liable to
lose a finger. Use the point of the curved Stanley blade to
score lightly round the sole outline. Then work the point in
deeper on the second, third, fourth, fifth, sixth time round,
etc. Keep the blade as vertical as possible. You can safely
use the knife the other way up now, point upwards,
carefully pulling it towards you along the half-made cut. If
you haven't cut vertically and exactly along the drawn lines
you'll have a lot of trimming and sanding to do later.
Leather shears are preferable to a Stanley knife when
cutting hide or latigo uppers. Again, turn your template
over for the second upper. If you are using a thinner leather
plus a skiver lining, cut the skiver fractionally smaller all
round than your template and your other leather about 1cm
bigger all round. The extra 1cm should be thinned by
skiving, then folded under and glued. You then glue and
stitch the skiver lining to the back. This is the same process
as that outlined for soft belts (page 88, figure 149).

Attaching uppers to topsoles Are you going to dye or
decorate the uppers and/or topsoles? If so now is the time to
do it, before you put them together. Do any riveting, sewing
or threading together of crossing straps now while you can
get at them properly. Soften the bits likely to chafe with
neatsfoot oil and/or saddle soap.

The next step is a compromise: skive the extension tabs of
the uppers, the tabs destined to be sandwiched between sole
and topsole, without weakening them. If skiving looks risky
pound them hard with a mallet to compress them.

Now roughen up the underside, the flesh side, of the topsole
and the sides of the tabs that will come into contact with it
when slotted through and folded under. Use a really fierce
wire brush to do this. Knock off all those loose particles.
Smear glue on the areas to be glued, wait until they're
tacky, then press them together (figure 221). Slide your
handiwork on to a last (or similar) and pound the joints so
that the glue penetrates their every pore and cranny.
Personally we find a line or two of saddle stitching through
the tabs and the topsole at various points very reassuring.
Use a mallet and round awl to make the holes.

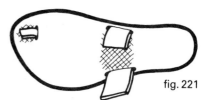

fig. 221

Attaching soles to topsoles Again the procedure is to roughen up your surfaces, knock the dust off them, smear them with glue, wait, press them together and hammer over every inch of the sole to create a lasting bond. The sole should have the grain side on the bottom, naturally. Sole and topsole will bond on contact if your glue is of the right tackiness, so put that topsole down exactly on top of the sole.

Finishing If you've cut out two perfectly identical pairs of soles and topsoles you're a genius. Usually there's a bit of paring to do with the curved Stanley or skiving knife. Then you rasp away all round the sides of the sandals with coarse glasspaper, graduating to fine for the final smoothing. (A power tool with an emery cylinder attachment does the job a lot faster, but don't dawdle or you'll burn the leather.) Bevel and dye the edges if that's the look you want. Get rid of the fuzziness by lightly damping the leather and burnishing it with something hard and smooth – a milk bottle comes in handy. Bring up the shine with beeswax and a lot of rubbing.

Buckles, usually the centre bar variety, go on next. Ankle buckles go on the outside of the foot – you don't want them clashing together as you walk. Slip the sandals on and mark two or three holes for the buckle prong in the thread-through straps.

The sole/topsole bond can be strengthened here and there, around the edges of the sole, for example, or through the tabs of the upper, with cobbler's nails. These are sharp pointed tacks with flat heads. The points curl up when they hit a metal last, preventing the nails slipping back the way they were banged in. Beg a handful from an obliging shoemaker or buy them (in rather large quantities, unfortunately) from a footwear supplies merchant. Choose tacks about 2mm longer than the full thickness of your sole or heel, and hammer them in from the topsole side. Bang them in gently, and vertically, to start with, ending with two good thumps to make the points curl round properly against the last.

Micro, resin or composition soles are a lot less slippery than leather ones. Usually, although not invariably, merchants who supply sole leather also supply non-leather sole sheeting of various kinds. So, if you're not a purist, go and buy a square foot or two (or find an obliging shoemaker to sell you some). Your alternative is to buy a gargantuan pair of stick-on soles and trim them to the right size. Use the sandals themselves as templates – by now they're probably slightly different from your original sole template. Roughen up both the leather and non-leather surfaces before gluing. Work over the whole sole with a hammer to strengthen the glue bond.

And now, a word about how the sandals in the photograph depart from the instructions given above. First of all, the decoration on the uppers: this consists of a cutwork panel appliquéd with single lines of saddle stitching, and a tassel over the big toe done before the upper/topsole joining stage. Second, we fancied having a false topsole in the same leather as the upper (thick 'side leather'). So we attached it to the topsole proper (4mm hide) with glue and a line of saddle stitching. See the stitching round the inside of the slots which take the uppers? It actually goes through the extension tabs of the uppers. The toe tab is firmly anchored in the same way.

Then the soles have two extra thicknesses of sole leather to make the low wedge heels. Figure 222 shows how these extra pieces looked before they were assembled. They curve at the instep end (a) because the arches need support farther forward on their inner side than on their outer. Skive the instep ends so that they form a nice smooth slope when you glue them together (b).

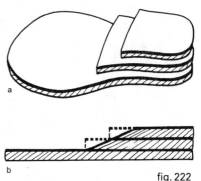

fig. 222

A last note for the ambitious. Sole leather can be soaked in warm water for about fifteen minutes and moulded to the sole of your foot, with a comfy hummock under the arch. Alternatively the arch area can be built up with cork or soling scraps sandwiched between sole and topsole. If you have your sights on high heels, higher than 3cm or so, that is, you'll need steel shanks to prevent the arches of your sandals sagging. Your local shoemaker may be able to help you here. If not, find out who his supplies merchant is. Heels can be built up from materials other than leather, of course, from micro or resin sheeting, wood or cork.

Clothes

This chapter isn't intended to be a crash course in dressmaking, though it may appear that way. Hopefully we've answered some of the questions you're likely to ask, like 'how do I flatten seams and hems if I'm not supposed to use an iron?', or 'what do I do with seams which are too bulky?', or 'help! my pattern pieces are too big for my leather'. We've assumed you will be working from a shop-bought pattern, Simplicity, Vogue, Butterick, McCalls and the like. All patterns give very clear and comprehensive instructions.

There is nothing difficult, no big mystique, about making clothes out of leather. In some ways leather makes the job easier – no fraying edges, for example. If you have successfully made clothes before, go right ahead. You know your level of expertise. Stay within it for your first leather job and leave Savile Row to the professionals!

Leather Garment cowhide finished for wear on the suede or the grain side, cowhide splits and nappa are the leathers most commonly used for making clothes. They come in a range of qualities and thicknesses. Unfortunately splits never wear as well as grain leather. On the other hand they can be easier to machine stitch. Chamois and buckskin are worth considering for softer styles. But think before you buy: suede shows the grime more than leather, so needs brushing and spot cleaning more often. Even once-in-a-while dry cleaning is expensive and will only give the best results on good-quality leather. So our advice is buy the best you can afford and look after it (see page 21) to save on dry cleaning.

Tools and things The pros and cons of hand and machine stitching are outlined on page 38, the thickness of your leather being the crucial factor. Apart from various needles and awls, if you're going to hand stitch, and a sewing machine, if you can get away with machining on the leather you're using, you'll need thread (Sylko 40 for machine sewing, and the same or linen or button thread for hand stitching), leather shears, glue, a mallet, sellotape, a biro and probably a tape measure.

Choosing a pattern Patterns for making clothes can be bought in most shops which sell clothing fabrics. Every pattern states the amount of fabric needed and gives detailed, illustrated instructions on cutting and sewing. Choose something simple if you're not too confident. All pattern catalogues have an easy-to-sew section.

If you find it hard to visualize a pattern on yourself, do some market research. Try on all sorts of styles until you find one or preferably two which do something for you. Go back to the pattern book. Would either of them work in leather? Bear in mind that leather has more body and less give than fabric and doesn't generally hang or drape as well. It can't be pressed with a hot iron either.

Look for raglan or kimono-type sleeves (figure 223a and b) rather than inset ones which need a lot of easing round the armholes (figure 223c). Look for A-line or wrap-around skirts rather than thigh huggers – they won't seat so easily. Look for trousers with seams just above the knee – they won't give at the knee so easily. Beware of gathers and darts if you're working with fairly substantial leather.

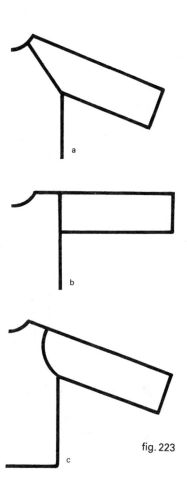

fig. 223

How much leather do you need? On the back of every pattern envelope there is a table which shows the amount of fabric needed in metres. Square feet, not metres, are what interest you, so you'll have to convert.

Suppose your pattern says you need 3 metres of 90cm-wide fabric 'without nap'. Well, there are $10ft^2$ in 1 metre of fabric this wide, so multiply the number of metres by 10, $3 \times 10 = 30$, and add a 20 per cent safety margin, $30 + 6 = 36$. That's how much leather you need, $36ft^2$. That extra 20 per cent is necessary because there is more waste in a skin, due to flaws and uneven edges, than in fabric.

If you have to convert from yards and a fabric width of 36in, use 9 as your first multiplier. Conversion factors for other widths are given in the Appendix.

Now, the 'nap' question. A sueded leather has a 'nap' if it looks dark when you smooth it one way and light when you smooth it the other. If your leather has an obvious nap convert from the 'with nap' requirement stated on the pattern envelope. This is always more generous than the 'without nap' requirement to enable you to cut your pattern pieces with the nap running the same way on all of them.

Adapting your pattern to your leather If your leather is very thin it is perfectly feasible to construct a garment exactly as you would a fabric garment, faithfully following the pattern instructions – no tricky business. When it comes to cutting out, cut along the heavy 'cutting lines' of the pattern. You're going to need the same seam allowances as you would for joining fabric.

The subtleties begin when your leather is thicker than, say, 1mm. Unless you are prepared to skive the edges of all main seams, fabric-type seams (usually variations on the plain seam, figure 40, page 35, and figure 224a) are to be avoided. They look far too bulky. Abutted seams (backed with tape or a strip of leather (224b)) or overlap seams (224c) are much better. If you decide on overlap seams eliminate the seam allowance (i.e. use the 'seam line' as your cutting line) from *one* of the edges to be joined. For abutted seams eliminate the seam allowance from *both* edges. To avoid total confusion mark the lines you intend to cut along in red felt tip pen. Darts are a problem with thick leather. Try replacing them with an overlap or abutted seam. This is how you do it: continue the line of the dart to the nearest edge of the pattern piece and cut the pattern piece into two (figure 225). Add a seam allowance to one piece if you want an overlap seam. Another case for minor pattern alteration is when your pattern pieces are too big for your leather, which happens quite often. Keep your cool – an all-in-one pattern piece for a tunic back could be cut as two, three or four pieces (figure 226). If you decide to use plain or overlap seams in a case such as this, add on some seam allowances.

Extra seams are a good idea in two other specific cases: just above the knee in trousers and just above the seat of a skirt (figure 227). Cut your pattern pieces in the appropriate place and if necessary add on some seam allowances.

When it comes to garment edges – front openings, neck openings, armholes, collar edges – the general rule is: keep all seam allowances if you want to turn the edges under in some way, and abolish them if you don't. It's safest to cut along the 'cutting line' for hems, sleeve ends and trouser bottoms, unless you're short of leather, and adjust the length when the garment is well on the way to completion.

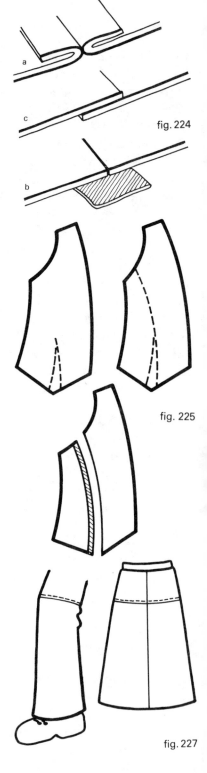

fig. 224

fig. 225

fig. 227

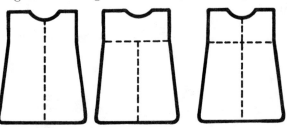

fig. 226

Does the pattern fit? The only way to make sure a pattern fits is to do a trial run, main seams only, in felt or muslin – felt is better because it behaves more like leather. Sew the pieces together with big running stitches, using the type of seam (plain, overlap or abutted) you intend to use on the real thing. Draw your alterations on the felt, then transfer them to the pattern.

Cutting out We prefer to cut along lines drawn in biro on the leather itself (on the wrong side) rather than along the edge of a flimsy paper pattern. You make a neater job of edges this way which is important if they are going to be visible in the finished article, as with overlap seams.
Take out any creases or wrinkles in your leather (see page 22) – this makes accurate pattern cutting easier.
Lay out the pattern pieces on the back of the leather, steering clear of any flaws which appear on the front, and stick them down at intervals with sellotape. The grain arrows on all the major pattern pieces should run from head to tail of the skin, not across it, and all the pieces should point the same way (figure 228). Carefully draw round each piece with a biro. Don't forget to mark the little triangular notches where the pieces match up. You'll have to turn your pattern over to mark the second arm, second front, etc. If you don't you'll end up with two right arms, and two right fronts! The stretchiest parts of a skin are to be avoided. As far as possible make sure that corresponding pieces (i.e. left sleeve, right sleeve) have the same amount of stretch, or firmness, on corresponding edges. If they haven't they tend to hang and wear differently.

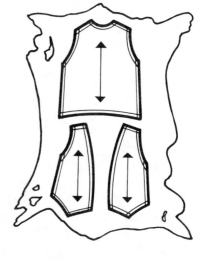

fig. 228

Hand or machine stitching? This is entirely determined by the thickness of your leather and the sort of thread you want to use. Thick leather and/or thick thread invariably mean a hand stitching job, unless you have access to an industrial sewing machine.
Domestic sewing machines are reasonably good-tempered on thin and medium weight splits but less so on grain leathers, especially if they're shiny and you're stitching with the shiny side down. A special 'easy feed' foot, available from most sewing machine shops, counteracts this problem to some extent. Please experiment with scraps first. Always use a leather needle (the thicker the leather the thicker the needle) and strong thread (Sylko 40). More information on machine stitching appears on page 38.
If hand stitching is the only answer you'll need the sorts of

threads and needles mentioned on page 36. Again the thicker the leather the thicker your needle needs to be. Where you're working with very thick leather or very thick seams pierce your stitch holes with a harness awl rather than the point of your needle. Leather needles have one big drawback, as we point out elsewhere: if you use the same stitch hole twice the sharp point cuts the thread of the previous stitch. Running stitch, the smaller the better, is the obvious answer, but it's not as strong as back stitch or saddle stitch or some of the more decorative stitches illustrated on page 37. A stitching awl is not really suitable for thin leather because one tends to pull the stitches tight to lock them, which results in rather strangled-looking seams.

Again, a few minutes experimenting can save a lot of snags.

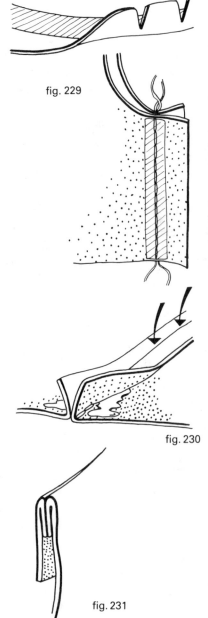

fig. 229

Taping seams and edges It pays to tape any edges and seams which are likely to stretch or receive a lot of strain. The thinner the leather the more important it is to do this. All you do is glue a length of thin non-stretch cotton tape to the wrong side of the leather along the seam line of one of the two pieces to be joined or, if you are turning a hem or flap, along the fold line (figure 229).

Prime candidates for taping are: curved edges (necklines, armholes, some hems) whether they are turned under, reinforced or faced; stretchy straight edges (hems, sleeve ends, main openings) whether turned under, faced or reinforced; seams which are expected to take a lot of strain (crutch seams in trousers, sleeve-to-armhole seams, especially in the armpit area).

Flattening seams, darts and edges Leather seams, etc. should be glued and then flattened with a mallet, not, repeat not, pressed with an iron. The drill here is: spread your glue sparingly, spread it close to the seam/dart/fold you are going to flatten, press the leather down with your fingers and tap over it lightly with a mallet, taking care not to hit the free edges of the seam/dart/fold (figure 230) or they'll show as ridges on the front of the garment.

fig. 230

Neck openings, armholes, jacket flaps Your pattern will almost certainly deal with these by the turned-in facing method (figure 231). This is fine if your leather is thin, though there's really no need to turn and stitch along the free edge of the facing. Trim a little off the seam and clip any curves so that the facing lies comfortably against the

fig. 231

inside of the garment. Glue the facing to the inside of the garment close to the seam and flatten the turned edges with a mallet. If you are working with thin leather tape the seam lines of the main pattern pieces before you attach the facings.

Turned facings look rather uncouth on thick leather, so we suggest you quietly ignore your pattern instructions and attach your facings to the outside of the garment (figure 232). If you do this you should cut off the seam allowance round the neck, armhole or whatever, and all seam allowances off the facing pieces. Outside facings kill two birds with one stone – they reinforce as well as decorate. If facings frighten you then just turn the edges to the inside, and glue and flatten them. Curved edges should be clipped (see page 44) and thick edges skived before you do this. But it's still a good idea to tape straight and curved edges if there's any likelihood of their stretching.

Bound edges (see page 44) are a perfectly acceptable alternative to facings.

Pleats The tops of pleats look good if you reinforce them with a little triangle of leather (the pleats of the pocket panel photographed on page 75 were reinforced like this). Pleat creases stay in pretty well if you work them over with a mallet. Put an extra piece of leather between the pleated edge and the mallet so as not to leave mallet marks.

Pockets Follow the pattern instructions, but don't try turning thick leather pockets under at the edges – just appliqué them (the right hand pocket in the photograph on page 75 was appliquéd with saddle stitch). Back and double stitch the top corners of pockets for extra strength (figure 233).

Hems and cuffs The simplest method of finishing hems and cuffs is not to finish them at all, but this looks rather nasty on all but the thickest leathers. Turning under, gluing and flattening is the most obvious solution, plus a line of stitching if you like. Many of the edge treatments discussed on page 44 are suitable as well.

But beware of edges stretching as you work on them. This happens because the bottom edges of your main pattern pieces probably follow the cross grain of the leather, the direction with the most stretch. So before you turn or bind or reinforce thin leather edges, tape the fold line (see 'Taping seams and edges' opposite).

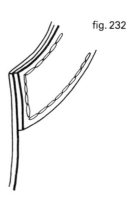

fig. 232

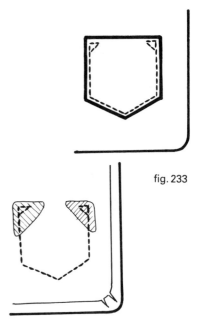

fig. 233

Buttons and buttonholes Always make buttonholes a shade longer than your buttons; always back buttons with other small buttons to prevent them ripping off; and always use button thread to sew them on. Self-cover metal buttons work very well with thin leather.

We favour the bound rather than the stitched type of buttonhole – stitched ones are a bit of a bore and they tend to stretch. The simplest type of bound buttonhole consists of a rectangular slot backed by two small pieces of leather, folded and glued double, which meet like lips in the middle of the slot (figure 234a). The lip pieces are stuck to the back of the slot, then you stitch round the slot through all thicknesses (b). (To make buttonhole slots in thin leather cut a V-ended slit (c), glue back the edges to make a rectangular opening (d), then proceed as above.)

Zips Your pattern will give full instructions on inserting zips. That said, zips can be inserted in the back of plain or abutted seams (figure 235a and b) – use small pieces of sellotape to hold the seam closed and keep the zip in place while you stitch. In overlap seams the neatest solution is to cut the leather away so that the zip shows on the front of the garment (c). Also there's no reason why you shouldn't sew the zip to the front of a garment and then hide the zip edges with braid or fancy cut strips of leather (d).

Other fastenings Don't restrict yourself to zips and buttons. What about lace-up openings, with eyelets and thonging, or various loop and toggle arrangements, or press studs?

Linings The function of a lining is to help prevent bagging and sagging, and rubbing or discolouring of the clothes you've got on underneath. Even so there are no rules about what to line and what not to line.

It's nice to see a lining in garments which flap open – coats, jackets, waistcoats – but not strictly necessary. The one place, in our view, where a lining really is *de rigueur* is in skirts. We've yet to see a pair of lined leather trousers though.

Cheap lining fabric rather defeats the object of the exercise, so go for quality and make sure it's non-crease and dry cleanable.

A lining should be a replica of the outer garment, minus any extra seams you put into your leather. You'll be using plain seams to sew the lining together, so reinstate any seam

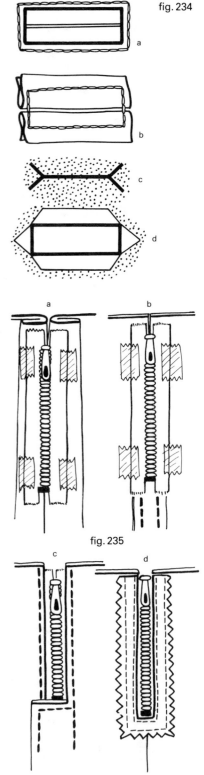

fig. 234

fig. 235

allowances you abolished on your leather. Paper clips are good for holding lining and outer garment together while you slip stitch the turned-under edge of the lining to the leather. Use a fine ordinary needle to do this – a leather needle will only cut the lining fabric.

Now, a few comments about the Waistcoat and Tunic photographed on pages 74 and 75.

Waistcoat

This is made of thickish leather, 1·5mm-thick garment cowhide. We decided to make the suede side the right side. The pattern we used had just two pattern pieces, back and front, plus the usual back strap, before we started altering it to suit our leather. We made all the main seams into overlap seams and did a double row of top stitching along each using a stitching awl and waxed linen thread. The darts in the front and back were converted into overlap seams by the method outlined on page 122.

All the edges – bottom edges all round, neck and front opening, armholes – were skived, turned under, glued, flattened with a mallet and finished with a line of machine stitching about 5mm from the edge. Only the neck and front openings were taped.

The inside pockets were an adaptation of the technique used for the buttonholes, the bound slot-and-double-lip type discussed opposite. This type of pocket has three parts: a top lip, a bottom lip which also makes the front of the pocket, and a back piece (figure 236). Step by step this is how each pocket was made: a square-ended slot about 1cm wide was cut in the waistcoat front; the lower lip piece of the pocket was glued in place on the wrong side of the waistcoat front; then a line of stitching was made along the bottom edge only of the slot, through all thicknesses; the upper lip was then glued in place, followed by the pocket back (glued around the edges only); then the top and sides of the opening slot were stitched, through all thicknesses; lastly the edges of the pocket back and front were stitched together. The whole process, which is much less complicated to do than to explain, is illustrated in figure 237 (a and b show wrong side, c and d right side).

Our working order for the waistcoat was as follows:

1 Skive all edges (but not main seam edges) on the wrong side.

2 Tape neck and front opening edges.

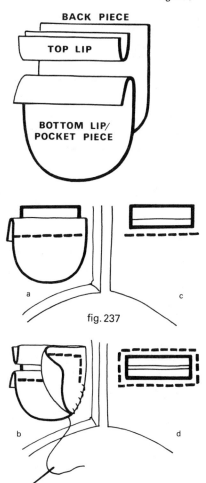

fig. 236

BACK PIECE

TOP LIP

BOTTOM LIP/
POCKET PIECE

fig. 237

3 Join dart seams by the overlap seam method, with a double line of saddle stitching along each.

4 Insert pockets.

5 Join side and shoulder seams (overlap seams and double top-stitching again).

6 Turn under, glue and flatten all edges, then machine stitch them.

7 Make the buttonholes.

8 Make the lining and slip stitch it to the inside of the garment around all edges.

9 Sew on the buttons plus small backing buttons, then slit the lining at the buttonholes, turn the edges of the slits under and slip stitch to the leather with an ordinary fine needle.

10 Sew on both halves of the back strap through all thicknesses, attach a small roller buckle and punch holes for the buckle prong.

Tunic

The salient points of the tunic are these: it is made of medium-weight cowhide split; it has raglan-type sleeves; it is stitched together by machine using the abutted seam method for the main seams; it has outside facings round the neck opening and sleeves; and it has a simple taped, turned and glued hem. The lacing around the neck and sleeves is purely decorative.

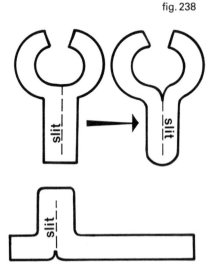

fig. 238

Originally our pattern had four pieces: tunic front, tunic back, sleeve, facing for neck opening. This is how we adapted it. First we eliminated all seam allowances from the main seams and from the neck facing, because we had decided to use backed abutted seams. Also, no matter how we shuffled the pattern pieces around, the tunic back could not be got out of a single piece of leather, so we cut it as two pieces, dividing it down the centre back line. Then we decided to round off the square corners of the neck opening, and all the square corners on the neck facing to match (figure 238). Then we thought the sleeve ends looked a bit boring so we decided to slash them to about 12cm above the wrist and concoct facings for them in the same style as the altered neck facing.

This is the order in which we did things.

1 Cut 3cm-wide strips of leather (same leather as the tunic itself) for backing all the abutted seams.

2 Stitch the two halves of the back together, then stitch all the shoulder seams (figure 239 shows the machine stitching details).

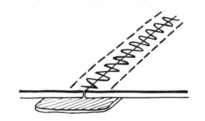

fig. 239

3 Glue, then stitch neck and sleeve facings to the outside of the garment with double rows of running stitch very close to the facing edges. NB. We did not cut the neck and sleeve slits until the garment was completed.

4 Stitch side and arm seams (abutted seams and the same machine stitching details as before). Actually it's impossible to stitch from the armpit to half way down the arm using a machine, so you have to hand stitch, imitating machine stitch as far as possible.

5 Tape all the way round the fold line of the hem, clip the curves, then turn and glue the edges under and flatten them with a mallet.

The coloured lacing around the neck and sleeves comes last of all. Each lace threads in and out of its own set of slits, cut through all thicknesses with a slit punch or chisel of suitable width. Arrange to join lacing lengths (see figure 38, page 34) on the back of your work. Go over the laced area with a mallet so that the laces lie nice and flat. The neck ties thread through small holes on either side of the neck opening and knot on the back. They also have bead ends.

Gloves and hats

Glovemaking is outside the scope of this book, but if you're neat with a needle, do have a go at making your own gloves – it's immensely satisfying. You'll find the address of a supplier of gloving leathers and glove patterns in the Appendix. The same goes for hats – one of the tool suppliers in the Appendix stocks hat patterns.

Furnishings

In the upholstery line there's little that can be done in fabric that can't be repeated in leather – the methods are basically the same. There are plenty of good books on upholstery so we won't attempt to outline the techniques here.

Upholstery cowhide is the best leather to use and this comes in a wide range of colours. However, it's only sold as full or half hides, and even a half hide can be 20ft^2 and upwards. So, if you're just refurbishing the odd chair seat it's more economical to use nappa instead. For pouffes or cushions either sort can be used, and on the whole a grain leather is more serviceable than suede.

fig. 240

Don't ignore the potential of thick hide. It's tough, durable stuff, perfect for making the type of unsupported seating shown on the next page. If you're working in 3–4mm-thick natural vegetable tanned cowhide, it can be stamped, carved, tooled or dyed, perhaps with different parts of a design dyed different colours. If you buy pre-dyed cowhide in a sober brown or black you could use a laced pattern to provide a touch of relief on an otherwise plain panel.

Pouffe

Pouffes and leather go together, like willow and cricket bats. There are round pouffes, squarish pouffes, triangular pouffes, oblong pouffes and pouffes which join together. All have a top and bottom the same size and one or more long pieces to make the sides. And they're all tightly packed with stuffing. A really pukka pouffe has two kinds of stuffing: a layer of soft stuffing, which fills every nook and angle of the top and sides, and a non-squashable core of coarse stuffing.

Lacing, weaving, appliqué, Italian quilting, and embroidery are fairly obvious ways of decorating pouffes. If your leather is fairly thick you could try stamping and antiquing it, but the results will be inferior to stamping on proper tooling hide.

The pouffe on page 49 has a reverse appliqué design on the seat, piping in the top and bottom seams and a three-strand plait round its middle. The appliqué part was machine stitched but the rest was sewn by hand.

Leather Soft, flexible grain leathers 1–1·5mm thick are best for pouffes – that means the firmer type of garment cowhide or nappa, or upholstery cowhide. Suede is not a good idea except for decorative detail. Avoid very stretchy leathers. Thicker leather, up to 2·5mm, can be used but you'll probably have to modify the way you put your pouffe together; i.e. use overlap rather than plain seams and perhaps lacing rather than stitching.

Tools and equipment Essentially a pouffe is a stitching job, requiring little more than leather shears, needles and thread. We backstitched the main seams using a single harness needle, making the holes with a harness awl as we went along.

If your leather is fairly thin have a go at stitching two, three and four thicknesses together (piped seams have four thicknesses, as shown in figures 44 and 45 on page 35). If your machine manages two you might not have to do everything by hand. If it manages three it will probably battle through four with some careful skiving. Try anyway. Actually, machining can turn out to be much more of a struggle than hand stitching and often inferior.

If you plan to lace your pouffe together you'll need a rotary punch, or a slit punch and mallet, to make the holes. For the soft stuffing use kapok or fibrefill. Sea-grass and hog's hair are good for the coarse part or core of the pouffe. We used a heavy duty zip for the bottom closure.

Other tools depend on the method of decoration you choose (see pages 65–71).

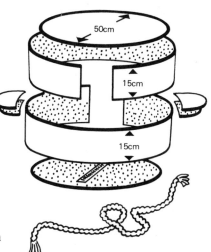

fig. 241

Pattern pieces The type of pattern we used for the pouffe in the photograph – identical top and bottom pieces, two long strips for the side walls and some 'ear' pieces (for hauling the pouffe around) – works for almost any shape of pouffe (figure 241). The plait (it could also be a strap or piece of stout cord) which cinches the waist of a pouffe is rather vital – it prevents middle-age spread!

Bottom closures You have a choice here, zip up or lace up. In either case the bottom opening should be as long as possible, about 5cm shorter than the width or diameter of the bottom of the pouffe. If you decide on a zip (make it a heavy duty one), cut a square-ended slot the length of the metal part of the zip and about 1·5cm wide. Glue the zip in place before you stitch. A round awl is best for making the stitch holes, as it won't tear the fabric of the zip. It also pays

131

to reinforce the ends of the zip with little pieces of leather (figure 242). For a lace-up closure you need only cut a slit, but it needs reinforcing with another piece of leather, preferably sewn as well as glued to the back of it (figure 243). The lace holes need to be strong, so reinforce them with eyelets.

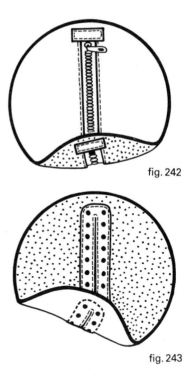

fig. 242

fig. 243

Putting the pieces together Having decorated your leather and made a lace-up or zipped opening in the bottom piece you can start putting your pouffe together. Backstitch is stronger than running stitch and quicker than saddle stitch. Plain seams turned to the inside, with or without piping in them, are a natural for pouffes made of thinnish leather.

You may have to think about thonging or lacing your pieces together if you're working with thick leather. Use paper clips or sticky tape to hold edges together while you punch the holes – that's the only way you'll get them matching up. Remember to include an 'ear' or two in one of your seams. In our case an 'ear' was two semicircles of leather seamed together round the edges and turned right side out.

Each strand of the plait which goes round its middle should be double thickness. We tied the plait ends and fringed them. If you use cord, knot the ends or finish them with a leather tassel. Strap ends could be buckled, like a belt.

Stuffing Working through the bottom opening, line the seat and sides of the pouffe with the soft stuffing, pressing it well into the seams. Pack in large, flat wodges rather than little knobs. Compress it as much as you can. Now fill the middle with the coarse stuffing, pushing it down and outwards until the leather skin is taught and firm. Zip up or lace up the bottom. Now secure your plait, cord or strap round its midriff. It should give a gentle sigh – 'poof!' – when you sit on it.

Bolster cushion

The only criteria for cushions are that they should be comfortable, beautiful and not fall to bits with a reasonable amount of squashing and pummelling. The sole representative of the genus in this book is photographed on page 49. It's a bolster constructed like the cardboard tubes you get inside toilet rolls and made of lengths of brown, grey and russet cowhide split laced together.

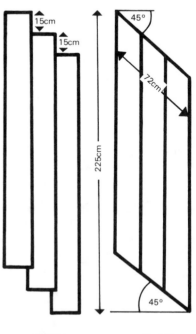

fig. 244   fig. 245

Leather Any soft, supple leather about 1mm thick is ideal for cushions. Whether you choose a grain leather or a flesh split depends on how much punishment you want your cushion to take.

Tools Leather shears, a drive punch and a lacing needle are all the hardware you need to make the bolster in the photograph. If you decide to stitch rather than lace the joins you'll need harness needles and a round awl and mallet for making stitch holes, or, if your leather is thin enough, a leather needle. Glue or sellotape is useful for holding seams together in readiness for lacing or stitching. The lacing used for the bolster was fairly firm, thin grain leather 3mm wide. If you use thread, use something strong like waxed linen or button thread.

Other tools will depend on how you intend to decorate your cushion. Chapters 9 and 10 tell you what equipment you need for the various techniques.

Making the bolster tube You need three strips of leather 15cm wide and 225cm long. That's pretty long so you'll probably have to join bits together; make diagonal joins and watch the direction of the nap if you are working with suede or splits. We use the abutted sort of join in this instance, with a strip of cotton tape glued to the back, and for the sake of speed we used machine stitching (the stitching details are those shown in figure 239, page 129).

Now place your strips together as shown in figure 244, overlapping the edges by about 2cm. Glue the edges together but don't spread glue over the whole width of the overlap – keep it away from the edge of the top strips. Next cut both ends at an angle of 45° – your cut edges should be approximately 72cm long, the circumference of the bolster when it's rolled into a tube (figure 245).

Now make your lacing holes and thread your lacing through them zigzag style (figure 246). The next step is to join the long edges of the panel to make a spiral tube (figure 247). Glue the edges together 30cm at a time as before, making your lacing holes and threading the lacing through them before you go on to the next 30cm. The final decorative touch on these main seams is to 'pink' them (figure 248).

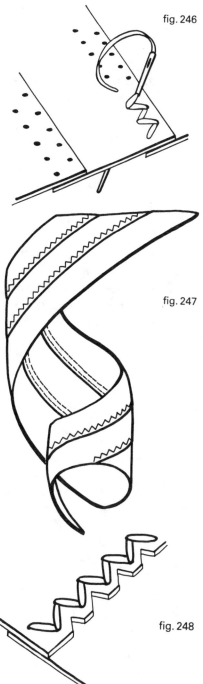

fig. 246

fig. 247

fig. 248

Finishing the ends The ends are tied closed with lots of laces, which then get threaded through a leather-covered half ball to make a tassel (see detail photograph, page 50). The original full ball can be of wood or polystyrene – we used a polystyrene one 7cm in diameter. Polystyrene is much easier to cut and make holes in than wood and is quite strong enough for the purpose.

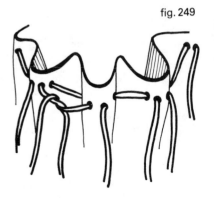

fig. 249

Make the lace holes in groups of four around both ends of the bolster (figure 249). Aim to get about 20 groups of four around each end. Then cut 40 lengths of lacing about 50cm long. Figure 249 shows how we threaded each lace through the sets of holes. As you tie the ends of each lace (use a granny knot) you gather a little bit of the bolster end. When one end is gathered as tight as you can get it, bind all the laces together as close to the bolster as possible. Now put in the stuffing. Repeat the lacing and gathering operation at the other end.

Next you cover both halves of the wooden/polystyrene ball with leather. You do this by gluing a circle of leather to the bottom, spreading glue on the hemispherical part and folding the leather up over it (figure 250). Cut away the excess leather and oversew the cut edges to form ridges. Glue the ends of the leather inside the hole and make a hole in the leather covering the base.

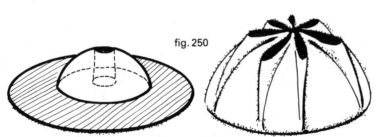

fig. 250

Now cut a circle of leather slightly larger than the diameter of the half ball you have just covered, pink its edges and cut a hole in the centre of it. Slide it over the lace ends so it lies flush against the end of the bolster. Poke all the laces through the hole in the half ball and push it tight up against the bolster. To keep it in place tie random pairs of laces together so that their knots lie in the hole. The pressure exerted by the knots against the sides of the hole keeps the half ball on.

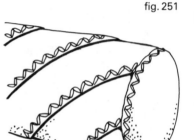

fig. 251

If you can't be bothered with this tassel-making operation we suggest you cut two circles of leather the diameter of the bolster and lace them onto the ends (figure 251).

Chair

This is photographed on page 49.

We're not suggesting you make a replica of it! We thought we'd use it to demonstrate two things: first, that you can use a nappa leather to re-cover a chair, and second, to illustrate another decorating technique. If you paint a design on leather using leather paints (see page 47), then quilt around the pattern (see page 69 for quilting hints) it gives the impression of some pretty tricky appliqué work. So, quite simply, we made up two painted, quilted panels and used them to re-cover the chair seat and back as per normal. Still on the subject of chairs, thick hide makes excellent unsupported seating. Use a fairly robust frame over which to stretch the leather. If it's a wooden chair you can screw, tack or bolt the leather round the sides. If it happens to be a chair that was cane-seated you can use the holes in the frame to lace on a seating panel (figure 252). If the frame won't take kindly to screwing or tacking you could lace, stitch or rivet the leather *around* it (figure 253). An interesting variation which can be used where there are four sides for fixing is to cut strips of hide to make a woven seat (figure 254). In all cases the edges of the hide should be really well finished (see page 41), and the back of the hide dyed if it's likely to show.

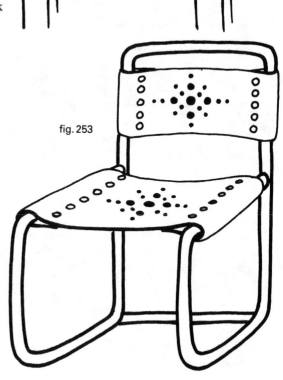

fig. 254

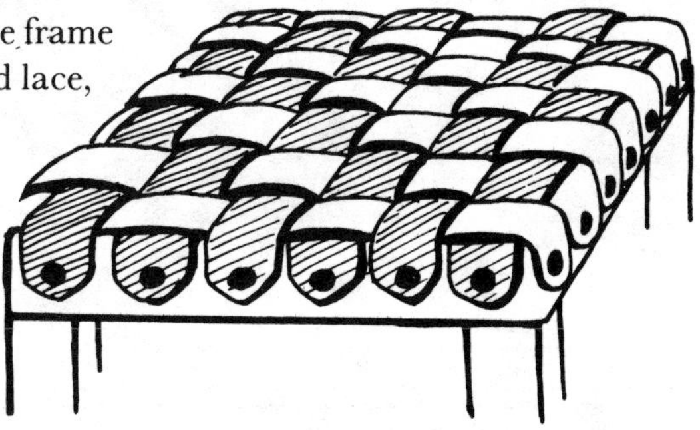

fig. 252

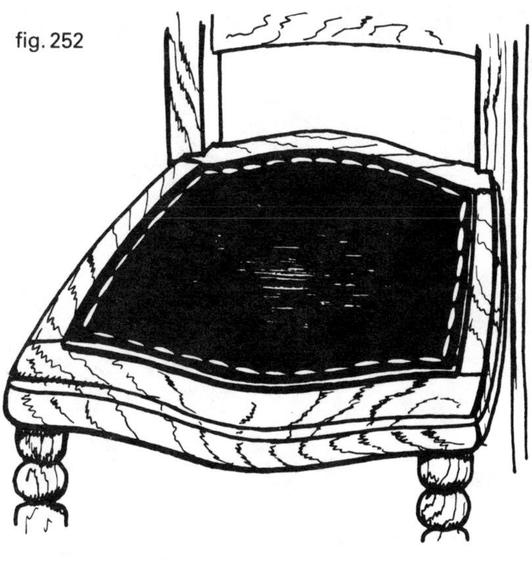

fig. 253

Carved screen

We carved and antiqued some 3mm-thick cowhide to make
the panels for the screen on page 49. The photograph on
page 52 shows the design in detail. Look at Chapter 8 for
information on how to carve.

Actually screens are quite a good vehicle for leatherwork.
You could fill panels with strap work in thick hide, plain or
woven (figure 255), try some cutwork (figure 256) or
perhaps use a piece of patchwork (figure 257).

Screens apart, leather carving could be used on any seat panel
or look effective on a waste paper bin or umbrella stand.

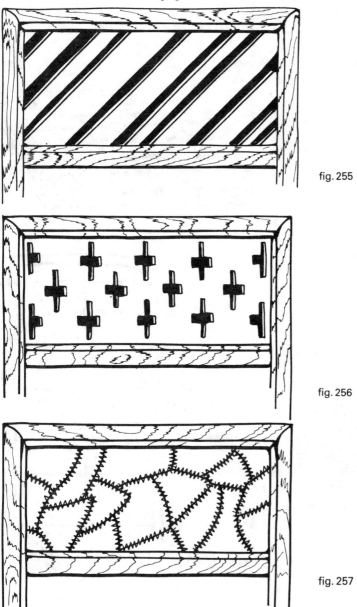

fig. 255

fig. 256

fig. 257

Appendices

Sharpening tools

Knives If you use a Stanley knife for all your cutting then you're laughing. Just replace the blades as they become blunt. If you happen to have bought some other knife for cutting leather or if you have a skiving knife then you'll need to put a good edge on it before you get to work. A newly-bought knife rarely has a fine edge – you have to give it one. Thereafter it'll just need sharpening occasionally to preserve the edge.

The first thing you need is a sharpening stone, sometimes called an oilstone, and the second is a small can of oil, 3-in-1 is fine. All DIY and tool shops are likely to stock both. A sharpening stone with a medium and fine side is usually best. If the knife has a really ropy edge start on the medium side of the stone, otherwise stick to the fine side.

Squirt some oil on the stone and lay the bevelled side of the blade flat on the stone. Then raise the blade ever so slightly to the angle of the bevel and work the blade round and round in little circles on the stone – some people work it backwards and forwards. If the blade has a bevel on both sides (e.g. a swivel knife) flip the blade over and have a go on the other side. Keep changing sides as the knife gets sharper. If you find you get a tiny loose edge of metal on the blade (you can feel it rough against your finger) strop the knife backwards and forwards on a piece of leather strap. Then get going with the oilstone again. If you're sharpening a swivel knife be extra careful that you preserve the angle of the bevels on the blade.

To finish the blade either strop it on a leather strap, or rub it in little circles on a piece of marble or plate glass. This polishes the blade and so reduces friction and drag when you cut.

Punches Here's how to sharpen the punches on a rotary punch, or any drive punch. Get yourself some fine emery cloth (not paper) – again try DIY or tool shops. Tear a small strip off the emery cloth, then holding the punch firmly (in a vice, get someone else to hold it, or grip it between your knees!) pull the emery strip backwards and forwards round the cutting edge. Work evenly all round the edge.

Edge beveller Sit the toe of the beveller on the fine side of the sharpening stone and work it gently backwards or forwards, or round in little circles. Make sure you preserve the rounded profile of the toe; it shouldn't become flat. Don't try and sharpen down the groove.

Groovers and gouges If the eye of your edge groover gets blunt, buy a replacement cross arm. The eye on a straightforward groover and the end of a race can, with care, be sharpened the same way as a punch. To sharpen a V-gouge work either side of the head on the sharpening stone – don't try to sharpen down the middle of the V.

Leather suppliers

All the companies listed here sell leather in small quantities. Ring or write for their catalogue or price list if you cannot call in person. All except one supply leather by post on a pre-paid, carriage paid basis. Their stocks change from time to time so ring them up before you order by post or call in person.

This is not an exhaustive list – for other suppliers look in your local Yellow Pages directory under 'leather merchants', 'leather dressers and finishers', 'leather manufacturers', 'tanners and curriers'.

J. & J. F. Baker & Co Ltd
Colyton
Devon EX13 6PD
tel 0297 52282

oak bark tanners; produce sole leathers, tooling hide, bridle and harness leathers; also sell bag hide and pigskin

Dougal Cameron Ltd
352 Leith Walk
Edinburgh
tel 031-554 2289

retail shops: sheep and calf leathers for clothing, shoes and fancy goods, sole leather and non-leather soling sheeting; also tools and sundries for garment-making

other Edinburgh branches at
51 Bread Street, 87 High Street
and 9 St Patrick Street

J. P. Milner Ltd
67 Queen Street
Hitchin
Herts
tel 0462 59618

merchants; specialize in gloving leathers (and glove patterns) but also sell good range of tooling hide, garment and handbag leather; also full range of tools, hardware, haberdashery, dyes and finishes, lots and lots of buckles, lacing and thonging, books

R. & A. Kohnstamm Ltd
Croydon Road
Beckenham
Kent
tel 01-654 3191

tanners; all types of leather, hide up to 3mm, public sales every six weeks or so on Friday evenings and Saturday mornings – ring for dates and times, personal callers only – do not supply by post

A. L. Maugham & Co Ltd
5 Fazakerley Street
Liverpool L3 5DN
tel 051-236 1872

merchants; clothing leathers (nappa, hunting calf, pig suede), bag hide, tooling hide; also sell some hide working tools, dyes and finishes

Alma (London) Ltd
Colton House
23 Charterhouse Square
London EC1
tel 01-253 6915

merchants; all types of leather (sheep, pig, goat, pony, hide up to 3mm) for clothing, travel goods, shoes and fancy goods

Connolly Bros (Curriers) Ltd
39–43 Chalton Street
Euston Road
London NW1
tel 01-387 1661

curriers; specialize in cowhide (tooling hide, case and bag hide, upholstery and garment cowhide, suede splits, bridle and harness leathers); also chamois

J. Hewit & Sons Ltd
97 St John Street
London EC1
tel 01-253 6082

tanners; specialize in bookbinding leathers; also sell bookbinding sundries

William Jeffery & Co Ltd
88–90 Weston Street
Bermondsey
London SE1 3QH
tel 01-407 1931

merchants; specialize in sole leather and leathers for shoe uppers, also tooling hide and non-leather soling sheeting

S. O. Rowe & Son Ltd
36–40 Tanner Street
Bermondsey
London SE1
tel 01-407 0735

tanners; specialize in reptile leathers, also goat (Morocco) and seal leathers for shoes, handbags and travel goods

Gomshall and Ass. Tanneries
Queen Street
Gomshall
Surrey
tel Shere (048 641) 2071

tanners and retailers; sheep leathers only, including nappa for clothing; also clothing patterns and a limited range of tools and sundries for making clothes

Suppliers of tools and equipment

All the suppliers below sell leatherworking tools and hardware. They also purvey that priceless commodity, advice, so ask away. Many will give you a demonstration of how to use certain tools, some even run leatherwork classes if there are enough people interested.

All of them sell tooling cowhide up to about 4mm thick and scraps or reject hides for practising on. Their stock of other leathers – nappa, garment cowhide, upholstery cowhide, cowhide splits, sole leather – varies. Some will order leather for you. Most sell kits of one sort or another and belt blanks. All have catalogues and do a lot of their business by mail order. Their stock changes from time to time, so ring up before you send in an order or pay them a visit.

The Cornish Sheepskin Shop
Boscawen Street
Truro
Cornwall
tel 0872 77396

full range of leatherworking tools including 6 carving tools, fancy stamps, fastenings, haberdashery, buckles, dyes and finishes, kits for bags and moccasins, books; leathers include tooling hide (no sole leather), some sheep leather and suede, belt blanks

The Leather Workshop
173a New Road
Parley Cross
Ferndown
Dorset
tel Northbourne (020 16) 4769

full range of leatherworking tools including carving tools, fastenings, fancy stamps, haberdashery, buckles, lacing and thonging, good range of dyes and finishes, kits; leathers include tooling hide (no sole leather), various garment and handbag weight leathers and suede but will order on request, belt blanks

Hobbie Crafts
Sackville Place
(behind Clearys)
Dublin 1
Eire
tel Dublin 722 877

full range of leatherworking tools, including carving tools, fancy stamps, fastenings, haberdashery, buckles, lacing and thonging, dyes and finishes, kits, wide range of books; leathers include tooling hide (no sole leather), various bag and garment weight cowhide and sheep leathers as available, belt blanks

Andrew Paterson & Co
12–15 St Andrews Square
Glasgow G1 5JJ
tel 041-552 1253

full range of leatherworking tools including carving tools, fancy stamps, fastenings, buckles, haberdashery, dyes and finishes, lacing and thonging, kits, books; leathers include tooling hide (no sole leather) and some sheep leathers

J. T. Batchelor & Co
146 Fleet Road
Hampstead
London NW3 2RH
tel 01-267 0593

basic leather working tools (no carving tools), fancy stamps, fastenings, haberdashery, excellent range of buckles and clasps, dyes (no finishes), some thonging; leathers include tooling hide, latigo cowhide, nappa, leather and sueded sides, pig suede, skiver, snakeskins, belt blanks

S. Glassner
480 Kingston Road
Raynes Park
London SW20 8DX
tel 01-543 1666

basic leatherworking tools (no carving tools), fastenings, turnlocks, buckles, general hardware, thonging and lacing, (no dyes or finishes); leathers include tooling hide (no sole leather); some handbag (no garment) leathers, splits (not clothing quality), skivers

Hidecrafts
9a Sheep Street
Skipton
North Yorkshire
tel 0756 60389

full range of leatherworking tools including carving tools, fancy stamps, haberdashery, fastenings, buckles, lacing and thonging, good range of dyes and finishes, own kits, moccasin patterns; leathers include tooling hide, sole leather, garment cowhide, cowhide splits, moccasin leather, some sheep leather, Morocco, belt blanks

D. A. Friend (Brighton) Ltd
28–29 Bond Street
Brighton
Sussex BN1 1RD
tel 0273 27607

full range of leatherworking tools including carving tools, fancy stamps, fastenings, buckles, haberdashery, dyes and finishes, some bookbinding equipment, lacing and thonging, kits, hat patterns, books; leathers include tooling hide, bridle leather, sole leather, latigo, range of clothing and handbag leathers, chamois, skivers, belt blanks

If you have difficulty locating suppliers of leather or tools in your area ring or write to the Leather Institute. Their address is:

Leather Institute
Leather Trade House
9 St Thomas Street
London SE1 9SA
tel 01-407 1582

Converting fabric requirements from metres and yards to square feet

For every metre of fabric 90cm wide, multiply by 10
                                115cm wide, multiply by 13
                                140cm wide, multiply by 15
                                150cm wide, multiply by 17
and add 20 per cent

For every yard of fabric 35/36in wide, multiply by 9
                                44/45in wide, multiply by 11
                                  54in wide, multiply by 13
                                58/60in wide, multiply by 15
and add 20 per cent

Index